Pickling Everything

THE COUNTRYMAN PRESS

A division of W. W. Norton & Company

Independent Publishers Since 1923

Pickling Everything

LEDA
MEREDITH

Foolproof Recipes for
Sour, Sweet, Spicy, Savory,
Crunchy, Tangy Treats

COUNTRYMAN KNOW HOW

Manufacturing by RR Donnelley Shenzhen
Series book design by Nick Caruso
Production manager: Lauren Abbate

Library of Congress Cataloging-in-Publication Data

Names: Meredith, Leda, author.
Title: Pickling everything : foolproof recipes for sour, sweet, spicy, savory, crunchy, tangy treats / by Leda Meredith.
Description: New York, NY : Countryman Press, a division of W. W. Norton & Company Independent Publishers Since 1923, [2019] | Includes index.
Identifiers: LCCN 2018036641 | ISBN 9781682681787 (pbk.)
Subjects: LCSH: Canning and preserving. | Food—Preservation. | LCGFT: Cookbooks.
Classification: LCC TX601 .M46 2019 | DDC 641.4/2—dc23
LC record available at https://lccn.loc.gov/2018036641

The Countryman Press
www.countrymanpress.com

A division of W. W. Norton & Company, Inc.
500 Fifth Avenue, New York, NY 10110
www.wwnorton.com

10 9 8 7 6 5 4 3 2 1

DEDICATION

This book is dedicated to my friend and fellow author Ellen Zachos. It was my pleasure to introduce Ellen to food preservation and foraging. It has been my honor to watch her turn those topics into wings and soar.

CONTENTS

Why Pickle?

(It's Not Just the Garnish for Your Sandwich)

Living up to the title, *Pickling Everything*, might seem either difficult or impossible. "Really, Leda?" you ask, *"Everything*?!"

Yes, really. You can pickle almost any whole food including vegetables, fruits, meat, eggs, and even cheese. By *whole food*, I mean foods that are themselves and don't have a slew of laboratory-created ingredients. For instance, you can pickle apples. You cannot pickle something with "apple flavoring" and a long list of ingredients you cannot pronounce (well, technically you could but . . . yuck!).

Historically, people likely pickled foods because pickling safely preserves fresh food that would otherwise spoil. And, perhaps, because it is one of the easiest forms of food preservation: it is so easy that none of the recipes in this book require canning (although many of them include optional canning instructions).

But pickling is more than a form of food preservation. It is also a way of turning mild-flavored ingredients into crunchy, tangy side dishes and intensely flavored condiments. Pickles can whet your appetite before a meal. That is one of the reasons that at restaurants in numerous countries around the world, an assortment of pickles often appears on your table before you even order. For example, sit down at a restaurant anywhere around the Mediterranean, and before you've even ordered, the table will be filled with spicy pickled peppers, turmeric-yellow pickled cabbage, olives, and glistening ruby slivers of pickled beets.

Pickles can cleanse your palate between courses, as with the Japanese *gari* (pickled ginger) served with sushi. Or pickles can help you digest a rich meal, as with Indian chutneys and Korean kimchi (yes, chutney and kimchi count as pickles). Many people all around the globe consider pickles an essential part of almost every meal.

Pickles are an easy way to preserve fresh food and a way to create wonderful taste combinations that enhance your meal. But there's more: pickles can even make us healthier. Of all the forms of food preservation, pickling is one of only two that I am aware of that have the potential to actually add health benefits to the food that the food did not possess in its raw state (more about that later). The second, non-pickling method, is dehydrating mushrooms in sunlight to increase their vitamin D content (yes, I'm serious).

Before we go any further, let's get clear on what I mean by "pickling."

According to the Merriam-Webster Dictionary, a pickle is an article of food that has been preserved in a brine or vinegar solution. (There is another definition listed, which is "a difficult situation," as in to be "in a pickle." I'm ignoring this last meaning.)

Hidden in that dictionary definition is the fact that there are actually two kinds of pickling. Pickles that start out in a light salt brine and then ferment themselves into an acidic food are one kind. Those that add an already acidic ingredient, such as vinegar, are another kind. This book includes instructions and recipes for making both types, and there is more information about both methods in the next chapter.

It may be a cliché to say that there is more you can do with pickles than just serve them alongside a sandwich (not that a pickle with your sandwich isn't absolutely lovely). But clichés start out with some truth, and the truth is that from the last quarter of the twentieth century until recently, Americans didn't do much else with pickles. I consider those decades brief, dark blips in the otherwise illustrious and multifaceted career of the pickle.

Fortunately, we have rediscovered pickles, and fallen in love with them perhaps even more than in any previous era of our history. There are now vendors at farmers' markets around the country selling pickles and nothing but pickles. In my old neighborhood in Brooklyn, NY, there are shops whose exclusive wares are jars of pickles. Pickling workshops sell out, and it is once again a custom to give a jar of your homemade pickles as a gift.

Probiotic fermented pickles, in particular, have become crazily popular. This is partly because of their health benefits. But I think it is also because making something so tasty with almost zero cost and no fancy equipment, simply by employing healthy bacteria to do most of the job for you, is sexy in a renegade way.

The probiotic (and prebiotic) components of fermented pickles such as Half-Sours (page 65) contain good-for-you bacteria similar to those in yogurt. The more we learn about the bacteria in our guts, the more we realize how important they are to our health. You could swallow a bunch of expensive pills from the health food store to get those probiotics . . . or you could make your own live food pickles that have the same health benefits and taste good to boot.

THE LOVELY CUSTOM OF JAR RETURN

It was an elderly lady named Lynette Muller who taught me the excellent tradition of always returning the jar after you finish the preserves someone gave you. I used to give Lynette a jar of homemade pickles or jelly on her birthday, and the jar always came back to me clean and ready to reuse. If she had time, she would fill the jar with something she'd made that was as yummy as what was originally inside. If she was short on time, she would simply wash and thoughtfully return the jar. This custom of giving back the jar dates from the Depression era (or probably even earlier), when fruits and vegetables could be had for free from the garden or farm but canning jars cost cash on the table. It is a lovely and practical way to show gratitude, and one I hope you will continue. It also lets the person who gave you the jar know that you ate up all of the homemade goodness inside it.

Raw, unpasteurized vinegar has similar health benefits, but even pickles made with pasteurized vinegar can be good for you. Research has shown that sour flavors increase saliva while we're chewing. Because our saliva contains enzymes that are the beginning of the digestive process, food with a sour flavor improves the way we digest anything eaten along with it.

So sure, it's great to enjoy a few pickles on your burger, but there are many other appetizing ways to incorporate these health-promoting foods in your daily meals.

17 WAYS TO USE PICKLES

Instead of Olives or Capers: The pasta recipe calls for capers, or the salad recipe calls for olives, and you have neither on hand. Not to worry: any of the pickles in the "Sassy Sour" section, chopped small if they are in big pieces to begin with, can provide a similarly tangy flavor boost.

Vodka Chaser: Pickled mushrooms are a classic treat in Russia, Poland, and many other countries as a quick bite after downing a shot of vodka. There is something about the two tastes briefly overlapping on your tongue that makes each both mellower and more flavorful. But mushrooms are not the only pickles you could serve this way: try the Mustard Zucchini on page 68.

Add to Mayo, Yogurt, Hummus, Sour Cream, etc. for Instant Dip or Spread: Stir any chutney, relish, or finely chopped pickle into a creamy base of your choice. Dig in with crackers, crudités, or . . . more pickles, such as cucumber, carrot, or zucchini spears.

Always on the Table Next to the Salt and Pepper: In Central America, the Middle East, Indonesia, and many other parts of the world, as soon as you sit down at a restaurant table, a jar of spicy pickled mixed vegetables appears on the table. One of the nice things about this custom is that people can follow their own taste preferences concerning how many of these piquant morsels to include in their meal.

Instead of the Onion, Celery, or Olive in Your Cocktail: Have fun with this one. How about a sliver of pickled beet to turn your whole martini magenta? Or the Pickled Carrots with Coriander and Ginger on page 42 instead of the usual celery in your Bloody Mary for a whole different taste experience?

As a Part of a Meze Spread: The Greek side of my family always included a colorful assortment of pickles on buffet tables that also included olives, good bread, dips and spreads, cheeses, and cured meats. Together these foods make a plentiful and delightful meal, no bulky "main course" required.

Bring Back the Relish Tray: Offer guests an assortment of pickles while they are waiting for their main meal. Choose a mix of colors, textures, and flavors for the most interesting spread, but do keep the pickle varieties separate (you don't want your sweet fermented cherries sharing juices with your pungent pickled peppers). Old-fashioned glass relish trays, with their shallow compartments, are perfect for showcasing your pickles. Look for them at secondhand and vintage shops. Keep in mind that vinegar

can send the taste of good wine askew, so if you are serving vinegar-based pickles, serve cocktails instead, and save any wine for the main meal after.

On Pizza . . . or Focaccia . . . or Pasta . . . or: Anything with a cheesy, buttery, or oily sauce might benefit from a wake-up dash of pickle juice or minced pickles. Pickled chile peppers are just waiting for you to invite them onto your pizza. And some chopped fermented pickles will not only taste as good as olives on your pasta, they will also help you digest it more easily.

As Their Own Sandwich, a la "Bread 'n' Butter": Pickles don't have to be the tagalong in your sandwich. Make them the main ingredient, and surround them with a milder-flavored support crew such as butter, mayonnaise, thinly sliced vegetables or meats, or pureed beans.

Palate Cleanser: I've mentioned the Japanese use of pickles as a palate cleanser elsewhere. That is a really great idea that has uses beyond the pickled ginger you're supposed to nibble between bites of sashimi. What if, between the soup and the main course, say, you passed around a plate of pickles chosen to clear the palate appropriately for the food to come? A small bite per person, and on to the next course . . .

Digestive Aid (if Fermented Pickles or With Live Vinegar and No Heat): Any time you serve live fermented pickles, you are going to make whatever is eaten alongside them easier to digest. No need to plan your entire meal around this. But if that meal is going to be especially rich and heavy (holiday time, maybe?), including a probiotic pickle somewhere in the feast is a considerate touch.

Soup Topping: Growing up, we always added a splash of vinegar to lentil soup just before serving. This tradition came from the Greek side of my family. Besides giving the soup a wonderful additional layer of flavor without overwhelming the other ingredients, I was told this made the lentils easier to digest. Especially if the vinegar was raw (unpasteurized), or the pickles fermented, that would have been absolutely true. But even just from a strictly flavor-focused standpoint, finely chopped sour pickles of any kind make an excellent soup topping. A dash of pickle juice is also good here.

Grilled Cheese Sandwiches: This is so simple I'm almost embarassed to include it, but a few slices of Hamburger Dill Pickle Chips (page 54) or Bread 'n' Butter Pickles (page 106) are the difference between a ho-hum grilled cheese sandwich and one that qualifies as total comfort food.

With Dip, Instead of Chips, Crackers, or Crudités: If the pickles are chunky or sturdy ones, such as zucchini or carrot spears, drain them in a colander and serve them instead of plain raw vegetables or other usual dippers.

As Part of a Chopped Salad: Add up to 25 percent chopped pickles to any chopped salad and you don't really need to add any dressing (a dash of olive oil at most). Try finely chopped pickled cauliflower with a raw carrot and daikon salad, or any sour cucumber pickle chopped and added to luscious ripe summer tomatoes with a bit of fresh dill. The potential combinations are infinite (let me know what favorites you come up with, because I'm sure I'll want to eat them).

Battered and Fried: Yeah, I had to go there. For really fabulous results, first blot the pickles completely dry and then treat them as the vegetable for tempura. Crazy good.

In Mayo-Based Salads (Tuna, Egg, Potato, etc.): Chopped Dilly Beans (page 46) in potato salad, Citrusy Celery Relish (page 136) in tuna salad . . . any mayonnaise-based salad I can think of perks up when you add a bit of pickle to it.

6 WAYS TO USE PICKLE JUICE

When you've polished off the pickles in a jar, what can you do with the pickle juice? "Pickle juice" is an old-fashioned term for the acidic liquid that was preserving the pickle. Pickle juice can either be the liquid left from a vinegar-based pickle or the liquid left over from a fermented pickle. Either way, it is good stuff that you do not want to throw out. Here are some ways to use pickle juice.

Salad Dressing: Use pickle juice instead of vinegar or citrus juice in any salad dressing recipe.

If Fermented . . . to Kickstart Another Fermentation: If the pickle juice is from a lacto-fermented recipe, see "Probiotic Pickles (the Lacto-Fermentation Method)" on page 20, you've got fermenter's gold. That liquid is alive and teeming with healthy bacteria that will almost guarantee your next batch of fermented pickles gets off to a successful start. Just add one or two tablespoons to the brine when you start your next ferment.

Marinades: Whether from vinegar-based pickles or ferments, the pickle juice is flavorful and acidic enough to use instead of the vinegar, citrus, wine, or other liquid in a marinade.

Bloody Marys and Dirty Martinis: A splash of pickle juice turns the ordinary into something special when it comes to these cocktails. And homemade pickle juice is almost always more multi-flavored and interesting than anything left over from a store-bought jar of pickles.

Pickleback: A shot of pickle juice served to chase a shot of whiskey. Self-explanatory.

To Brine Meat or Poultry: Add pickle juice to a brine recipe instead of any vinegar or citrus juice that might be in the recipe. Or use nothing but pickle juice to brine meat or poultry.

HOW TO TURN A PICKLE INTO A SPICE

I want to mention one more unusual way to use pickles, and that is to turn them into a dried, powdered spice. The flavors will vary, of course, depending on what kind of pickle you start out with. But count on a tangy spice in sprinkle-ready form. Pickles I have successfully turned into dried spice have included several kinds of kimchi, pickled mustard seeds, and pickled beets.

To make a zesty, unique, powdered seasoning, dry thinly sliced pickles or a thin layer of relish in a dehydrator or in an oven on its lowest setting. (If your oven's lowest temperature is anything higher than 150°F, prop the oven door open with the handle of a wooden spoon). Once they are crunchy dry, grind the dehydrated pickles in an electric coffee grinder or have at them with a mortar and pestle. Store in tightly sealed glass jars and use within 6 months (after that, the flavor starts to fade).

HOW TO USE THIS BOOK

Most of the recipes in *Pickling Everything* are for small-batch preserving. Sometimes the "batch" is just one jar. But all of the recipes in the book can be multiplied if you feel like diving in for an old-fashioned big-batch pickling blitz.

Pickling Everything is primarily organized by flavor rather than by food preservation method. For example, you'll find hot, spicy pickle recipes in the same chapter together, even though some of those recipes are vinegar-based and others are lacto-fermented. Sweet and sour pickles are similarly grouped in one chapter. In a few cases, an ingredient type (such as fruits, seeds, or animal products) determines what is in the chapter.

You will find that preparation times, optional canning times, and wait times have been given for each recipe. The preparation times are approximately how much active kitchen time you can expect to put in for that recipe. In regular cookbooks, the preparation time is usually listed separately from the cooking time. Because many pickles require no cooking time whatsoever—but some do—I've combined chopping and mixing, etc. with cooking time (if there is any).

Although any of the recipes in this book can be simply stored in the refrigerator, for those recipes suitable for canning and storing at room temperature in sealed jars, I've included canning instructions and processing time. Where I have not included a canning time, it is because that recipe is not suitable for canning.

Because these are pickle recipes, they are almost always going to need additional days, weeks, or even months for the flavor to fully develop. The wait times for each recipe let you know how long it will be until you can serve that particular pickle (or present it as a ready-to-be-eaten gift).

Occasionally a recipe gives ratios rather than precise measurements. These are the *best* recipes for preserving odds and ends from your garden or leftovers from your Community Supported Agriculture (CSA) share, or just what's hanging around in your refrigerator after your last shopping trip. They are also often the best recipes for foragers, who can't always predict precisely how much of this or that wild ingredient they're going to find.

What Makes Pickling Safe?

Pickling food does two things: it creates a new, usually tangy taste the food didn't have on its own and it preserves the food for much longer than it would have lasted if it hadn't been pickled. But how does it do that? How does pickling successfully defy mold, dangerous bacteria, and decay? How can pickling so perfectly preserve almost every kind of ingredient, from cheese to cucumbers?

The answer is actually quite simple. It is all about pH. But the fact that there are two radically different ways to pickle a food can be confusing. You need vinegar to make pickles, right? Not necessarily. It's a ferment, right? Sometimes.

UNDERSTANDING THE TWO KINDS OF PICKLING

It used to be that when you said "pickle," many people would just think of the sour spear of cucumber that came with their sandwich ... and not give much thought to how that pickle was made. But nowadays, when people hear "pickle," they are just as likely to think "probiotics" as they are to imagine a sour cucumber that came out of a jar.

What is confusing is that there are actually **two completely different ways to make pickles**. There is one that brings with it probiotic health benefits, and one that does not (but don't give up on that second method—it has its own benefits).

Both pickling techniques safely preserve food by immersing it in a liquid that has an acidic pH.

Don't let the fact that sometimes the initial brine is salty a.k.a. alkaline confuse you: the end result with pickles is always acidic. The method of creating the liquid that preserves the food may be through fermentation that begins with salt, or by adding an already extremely acidic ingredient such as vinegar. With both fermented pickles and vinegar-based pickles, the low pH of the final liquid the food is immersed in ultimately preserves the food. Whether through fermentation or the addition of an acidic ingredient such as vinegar, the end result is called a pickle. But as I've mentioned, the process of making these two kinds of pickles is very different.

Here is what you need to know about the two methods of pickling, lacto-fermentation and vinegar-based.

Probiotic Pickles (the Lacto-Fermentation Method)

I am willing to bet that you have fermented ingredients in your kitchen right now, whether you know it or not, and I am not talking about the obvious ones, such as beer and wine. Fermented foods include chocolate, vinegar, soy sauce, miso, and bread. Many pickles are fermented, including traditional kosher deli pickles, Korean kimchi, and sauerkraut.

Fermentation is one of the oldest forms of food preservation, and it predates canning by many thousands of years. In fact, canning and fermented

WHAT IS A PICKLE?

By definition, a pickle is 1) a piece of food, especially a cucumber, that has been preserved in a solution of salt water or vinegar; 2) a mixture of salt and water or vinegar for keeping foods: brine; 3) a difficult or very unpleasant situation.

For our purposes, I'm ignoring the third definition.

The origin of the word *pickle* points directly to salt-based fermentation rather than vinegar pickling. It comes from either the Dutch word *pekel* or the German word *pókel*, both of which can be translated as "brine" or "salted."

foods are poor partners. If you were to expose fermented foods to heat by canning or cooking them, you would kill off their lively, good-for-you, probiotic bacteria. For that reason, I do not recommend canning fermented pickles unless you absolutely *must* store them at room temperature for longer than a few weeks (otherwise, they need to go in the fridge or a *very* chilly garage or cellar).

My vegan friends shouldn't be alarmed about the "lacto" in the term lacto-fermentation. There is no dairy involved whatsoever. The term comes from the fact that lactic acid is created as a byproduct of the fermentation process. That lactic acid is also what gives lacto-fermented foods such as sauerkraut their signature taste: sour, but usually in a much lighter way than the sharp taste of vinegar-preserved pickles.

Fermented pickles are probiotic. What does that mean? It means that they are literally alive with bacteria that are essential to our health. The lacto-fermentation method eliminates bacteria that could be dangerous for us to consume, but encourages the growth of bacteria that are good for us.

Most people are familiar with the idea of "healthy bacteria" because of yogurt. You know that part of the label on store-bought yogurt that reads "with active cultures," or "with live cultures"? Those are euphemisms working hard to evade the word *bacteria*, because for most people that word has negative connotations.

People spend a lot of money on probiotic bacteria in pill form, and with good reason: Probiotics are credited with keeping digestive and immune systems healthy, reducing inflammation, speeding recovery from yeast infections, and possibly even preventing certain forms of cancer. But you could save some money by creating your own probiotic products through natural fermentation. Bonus: your probiotic pickles taste great, and eating them is much more fun than taking expensive pills. Not only that, the vitamin content of many foods actually increases when they are fermented, especially the amount of B vitamins. And as if all that weren't enough, lacto-fermented foods are easier to digest than raw

foods because the fermentation process is a kind of predigestion of the food.

LACTO-FERMENTATION: HOW IT WORKS

Put some chopped-up vegetables in a clean but unsterilized jar. Pour a simple salt and water brine over them. Leave the jar out at room temperature for a few days (or weeks, or months), then transfer it to a cool but not freezing place. That is almost all you need to know about how to do lacto-fermentation.

Yes, you read those instructions correctly: You do not have to sterilize the jars. And you do leave the food out at room temperature for days. You do not blast away bacteria with high heat by canning

WHAT IS A BRINE?

Most people think of salt when they hear the word *brine*, but in many pickle recipes it is common to see vinegar-based, spiced liquids also referred to as brines. Since the dictionary definition of *brine* is "a strongly saline solution," I've tried to avoid calling vinegar-based pickling liquid *brine* in this book. I may slip now and then, though, since it is a culturally ingrained habit. But I've tried to stick with brine for salty, first-stage lacto-fermentation liquid and *pickling liquid* for the kind that adds vinegar right at the start.

the food after it has fermented. And it is a safe and super-healthy form of food preservation.

Here is how lacto-fermentation works, and why it is safe. (More detailed instructions are included with each of the fermented pickle recipes in the book.)

Say *bacteria* to most people and they will immediately think of microscopic organisms that can be dangerous, even lethal to the human body. Quick! Grab the antibacterial wipes; nuke that infection with antibiotics!

But there are some bacteria that not only do not harm us but actually make us healthier. Recent research shows that we actually could not live without the beneficial bacteria that are always present inside our bodies. Right now, as you are reading this, there are millions of bacteria in your body working to keep you healthy.

Lacto-fermentation works because it creates extreme pH environments, both at the start and the finish of the process (although there isn't necessarily a "finish" to the process since fermentation will continue, even in your refrigerator).

Lacto-fermentation recipes usually start with a salty (alkaline) brine. The salt kills off potentially dangerous bacteria. Luckily, there are beneficial-to-us bacteria that can survive the salt brine. The bad-for-us bacteria are killed off by the salt in the brine, but the good-for-us bacteria are still there, alive and ready to get to work. The entire process is possible thanks to several salt-tolerant bacteria species within the genus *Lactobacillus*.

Okay, so the bad bacteria have been killed off by the salt, but the good salt-tolerant bacteria have survived. What next? Those good-for-us bacteria will work on the food, in a way pre-digesting it for us. During that process of fermentation, the environment in the liquid around the food shifts from the alkalinity of the original salt brine to something too acidic for any harmful-to-us bacteria to survive. This means that while an alkaline environment took care of any dangerous bacteria that were present when we first started making the pickle, the acidity created by the fermentation zaps any harmful bacteria that might get introduced later on.

The good-guy bacteria responsible for successful lacto-fermentation exist on the surface of vegetables and fruits. As I've mentioned, in most lacto-fermentation recipes the fresh food is covered in a salty brine. There are some vegetables that are so naturally salty that there is no need to add anything but plain water; see Fermented Beet (or Chard) Stems on page 242. The salty brine begins the elimination of harmful bacteria that are not as salt-tolerant as *Lactobacillus* and encourages the latter to start fermenting the food. During the fermentation, the *Lactobacillus* bacteria convert lactose and other sugars in the food into lactic acid. That's why the process is called "*lacto-fermentation*." The lactic acid creates a low pH (acidic) environment in which any new harmful bacteria that might show up cannot survive (and the lactic acid is also what gives lacto-fermented foods their characteristically tangy taste). Basically, the probiotic bacteria take over the neighborhood and make it inhospitable to other, less-friendly-to-humans bacteria.

WHAT TO EXPECT DURING FERMENTATION

Within a day or two, at room temperature, you'll start to see some bubbles on the surface of the brine the food is submerged in. The liquid will change from resembling clear water to having a slightly cloudier look (but it should *not* be completely cloudy, nor at all slimy—these would be signs that the fermentation went awry). The ferment (as such pickles are sometimes called) will develop a pleasantly light sour smell (think mild dill pickles).

Once these changes signal that fermentation is underway, you will transfer your ferment to someplace colder than typical room temperature, such as your refrigerator or an unheated cellar or basement. Fermentation will continue, but it will be greatly slowed by the colder temperature. This means that your fermented foods will keep their texture longer than they would if they continued to ferment quickly at warm temperatures. This is especially important when crispness is part of the culinary profile of the food, as it should be with whole dill cucumbers or fermented radishes, for example. But the fact that fermentation continues, albeit slowly, even in your refrigerator also means that the taste of your ferments will get more sour over time. If you discover that you prefer the lighter flavor of a recently made ferment, make small batches and plan on eating them within a few weeks. If you want a bolder taste, wait as long as several months before digging in.

One last note about fermented pickles and flavor: the impact of any spices or seasonings you put in will also increase, the longer you store your pickle. If you threw in some chile peppers, expect the fire to get hotter; garlic will become more pungent, and the taste of just one or two whole cloves can eventually override all other seasonings in the recipe. This can happen with vinegar-based pickles as well. It is for this reason that some of the recipes in *Pickling Everything* call for straining out or otherwise removing the seasonings at a certain point.

ABOUT STARTER CULTURES FOR FERMENTS

A starter culture for fermented pickles is simply a spoonful or two of liquid that is already teeming with the salt-tolerant *Lactobacillus* bacteria you need for lacto-fermentation. With two exceptions, it is not essential to add a starter culture to your ferments, although doing so can quicken the start of active fermentation. The exceptions are if you are fermenting a pre-cooked food, such as the Spicy Fermented Chickpeas on page 224, or if the food you intend to ferment was dehydrated, as with the Fermented Sundried Tomato Pickle on page 94.

Starter cultures can also help ensure a successful ferment if you've opted not to use any salt at all. They can be useful to prevent the food from spoiling rather than fermenting when the ambient temperature is warmer than 75°F.

Keep in mind that even if you don't use a starter culture, the fresh food itself will bring plenty of probiotic *Lactobacillus* bacteria to the party. But if you are leaving out salt, as in the Fermented Beet (or Chard) Stems recipe on page 242, the extra probiotic bacteria introduced by a starter culture will slant the odds in favor of a successful fermentation.

You can make your own starter either by simply saving a spoonful of the liquid from a previously successful ferment or by making whey from yogurt (see box). To use your starter culture, simply add some to the jar or crock with your next lacto-fermentation recipe. I use 1 to 2 tablespoons of starter culture per pint of water or brine.

DON'T USE PLAIN TAP WATER

If your tap water is not coming from a well or spring, it is almost certainly treated with chlorine, as well as with other chemicals such as fluoride. The chlorine is added—just as it is to swimming pools—to kill bacteria. It kills off bacteria so effectively that it can kill off the probiotic bacteria your fermentation depends on. Instead of a healthy, tasty, pickle, what you'd end up with would just be rotten, potentially hazardous food.

A simple water filter such as Britta is sufficient to remove enough chlorine and other chemicals to render even most municipal tap water useable for fermentation. Alternatively, you can leave an open pot

HOW TO MAKE A WHEY STARTER CULTURE

Strain plain yogurt through a cloth bag, coffee filter, several layers of cheesecloth, or a clean dishtowel, and you end up not only with thickened, Greek-style yogurt but also a mostly clear, yellowish, liquid. That liquid is whey, and it is loaded with lively *Lactobacillus* probiotic bacteria that can kickstart your fermented pickles.

or bowl of water out for 24 hours and the chlorine will evaporate. (I remember doing this for our aquarium fish when I was a kid. They didn't like the chlorine any more than the *Lactobacillus* bacteria do.)

Note that this question of chlorinated vs. non-chlorinated water is not as much of an issue for vinegar-based pickles. It may slightly affect the taste of your pickles, but it is not a safe food preservation factor.

ABOUT TEMPERATURE AND FERMENTATION

Fermentation proceeds more quickly in warm temperatures. Potentially harmful bacteria and mold also tend to thrive in warmer climates. What this means is that a fermented pickle you make in an unheated room in November may take longer to get going than one you make in the same room in July (unless you've cranked up the air conditioning).

One thing you can do to adjust for the effects of ambient temperature on your team of probiotics is to add slightly more salt (about ½ teaspoon per pint jar) if temperatures are above 75°F.

Ambient temperature is not an issue for vinegar-based pickles.

Vinegar-Based Pickling

Vinegar-based pickling liquids demolish harmful bacteria and mold right off the bat by drowning them in the acidity provided by the vinegar. This kills off not only potentially harmful bacteria but also the healthy-for-us probiotic bacteria that make the lacto-fermentation process work. There are advantages to vinegar-based pickles, most noticeably consistency: unlike fermented foods, vinegar-based pickles are relatively unaffected by ambient temperature or whether or not your water is chlorinated.

Note that there are two types of vinegar pickles: those that *must* be refrigerated, and those that may be either refrigerated or canned, depending on how you intend to store them. The difference is in the percentage of vinegar used in the brine.

To make it easy to figure out whether or not you've got enough vinegar in your brine to safely can your pickles, start out with vinegar that is 4.5 percent acetic acid or higher. Almost all commercially sold vinegars are in this range, and each brand lists the acetic acid percentage on the label. Homemade vinegar can be tested to confirm its acetic acid level.

Vinegar-based pickles are only safe for canning in a boiling water bath (page 28) for long-term storage at room temperature if 1) you started out with vinegar that was 4.5 percent or higher acetic acid and 2) you did not dilute it by more than an equal amount of water or other liquid. Or to put it another way, your final recipe has a pH of 4.6 or lower. (I'm aware that you could do the calculations with vinegars of differing acetic acid percentages to arrive at that low-enough pH. Go for it, if you are that kind of pickler.)

If you used more water than vinegar in your brine, your pickle is not a candidate for canning. You need to keep it refrigerated, and it will be the combination of acidity and cool temperatures that preserves the food. In fact, one of the advantages of refrigerator pickling is that you can use less vinegar than in canning recipes, thus creating a lighter, less pungent flavor.

Most commercially sold vinegar is pasteurized, but it is possible to buy live, sometimes called raw, vinegar "with the mother" (the mother of vinegar is a layer that contains vinegar bacteria). As with probiotic fermented foods, live vinegar has numerous health benefits, most directly for our digestive systems. But if your recipe calls for boiling the vinegar before pouring it over the other ingredients, then your vinegar is no longer live. That doesn't mean it won't make great pickles, just that it won't have the extra healthy properties the vinegar's label claimed.

You can make your own delicious vinegars from fruit scraps and peels (see "Something for Nothing," page 237).

HOW TO SAFELY USE HOMEMADE VINEGAR IN PICKLING

Most food preservation books and websites warn that it is not safe to use homemade vinegar in pickling. That is not true. Commercial vinegars are deemed safe for pickling because they contain at least 4.5 percent acetic acid, and almost all vinegar-based pickle recipes are based on that level of acidity or higher. Therefore, if you know the pH of your homemade vinegar, and it is acidic enough, there is no reason not to use it.

You can figure out the percentage of acetic acid in homemade vinegar with something called an acid titration kit, available from winemaking supply companies (see "Useful Resources," page 256). The process for testing for acetic acid is slightly different from the instructions the kit supplies for testing wine acidity. Here's how you do it (all of the tools and solutions come with the kit):

1. Use the 20 ml syringe that comes with the kit to measure 2 ml of homemade vinegar, and transfer that to the testing cup.
2. Add 20 ml of water and 3 drops of the indicator solution. Stir to combine.
3. Fill the syringe with 10 ml of the standard base solution. Add it to the mixture in the testing cup, 1 ml at a time. Stir after each addition. At first, the solution will be clear, but eventually it will turn dark pink. Stop adding the standard base when that happens.
4. Look at the syringe that held the 10 ml of standard base, and note how much you used up. For instance, if there are 2 ml left, then you used 8 ml.
5. Multiply the number of milliliters of standard base you added by 0.6. The result is the percentage of acetic acid in your homemade vinegar. For example, if you used 8 ml of standard base, multiply 8 by 0.6 and you get 4.8—4.8 percent acetic acid is safe to use for pickling!

Note: you are testing the acetic acid percentage here, not the pH. It can be confusing, because with acetic acid testing, the higher the percentage number, the more acidic the vinegar. But with pH testing, *lower* numbers indicate greater acidity.

TO CAN OR NOT TO CAN

Many pickles are acidic enough (4.6 pH or lower) that you may safely can them in a boiling water bath without the fancy equipment required for pressure canning. But should you? When should you bother with the extra step of canning?

The answer is mostly about storage space: **canning allows you to safely store wet foods (such as vegetables in pickling liquid) at room temperature.**

That means you don't need to refrigerate them (before opening, that is—you do need to refrigerate after the vacuum seal created by canning is opened, just as you would with store-bought pickles). Canned pickles will remain safely preserved indefinitely until opened. If your fridge is overloaded and your freezer already crammed, canning enables you to simply stash those jars of pickled peppers in a kitchen cabinet, or anywhere you have room (I once lived in such a small apartment that I had to store my home-canned foods under the bed . . . but that's another story). Canning also enables you to give away jars of your homemade pickles as gifts without the need to tell the recipient that they need to be put in the refrigerator immediately.

The downside is that canned pickles are often mushier than other kinds because the high heat they are subject to during canning basically cooks them.

Remember that only pickles that have a pH of 4.6 or lower may be safely canned in a boiling water bath (page 28). Pickles that are live ferments or that don't contain enough vinegar for a 4.6 or lower pH need the additional food preservation insurance of cold temperatures and should be stored in the refrigerator . . . or a cool cellar if you're lucky enough to have one.

Even with pickles that do have a low enough pH for safe boiling water bath canning, there are at least three good reasons *not* to can them:

1. **Don't Kill the Healthy Stuff**: The first reason to skip canning would be if the pickles are the lacto-fermented type. Fermented pickles are loaded with healthy probiotics, and canning utterly destroys the health benefits of such foods. Even if your fermented pickle tests acidic enough for boiling water bath canning, don't do it.

2. **Mushiness:** The second reason is that the heat of even a short canning process changes the texture of pickles. All pickles will lose some crunch during canning, even if you add pickling chemicals that are supposed to prevent that from happening.

3. **100 Percent Vinegar Means You Can Skip It:** If your pickles are preserved in full-strength, undiluted vinegar with an acetic acid content of 4.5 percent or more, you can safely preserve them at room temperature even without the

Canning was not invented until 1850, but pickling has been around since at least 2500 BC, probably longer. Before canning (and refrigeration), storing pickles safely depended mainly on storing them in cool places, such as underground cellars. Most American homes no longer have cellars. The refrigerator has replaced the cellar for most people, and canned goods, whether from the store or homemade, have made cold storage less essential.

added protection of a vacuum-sealed canning lid. Keep in mind that if your vinegar is "raw" (unpasteurized), it is a live product that will continue changing with time (usually getting more sour, and possibly developing a vinegar "mother"—more about that later).

To sum up, recipes that have a pH of 4.6 or lower may be safely canned in a boiling water bath. The advantage of canning is that you can store the sealed jars at room temperature for long periods of time (years). Pickles that are live ferments—or that have the low acidity of a pH higher than 4.6—need the additional food preservation insurance of cold temperature storage and should be kept in the refrigerator instead of being canned.

HOW TO STERILIZE JARS (AND WHEN NOT TO BOTHER)

If the recipe calls for processing in a boiling water bath for less than 10 minutes, you *must* sterilize the jars before filling them with food. To put that another way, for recipes that will be processed in a boiling water bath for 10 minutes or longer, it is not necessary to sterilize the jars (although they should be completely clean).

To sterilize canning jars, put them into your canning pot and completely cover them with water. Bring the water to a boil and leave the jars immersed in the rapidly boiling water for 10 to 15 minutes. Don't start timing until the water has reached a full boil. Do not boil the canning lids, because that could ruin the adhesive ring. Once the jars have finished sterilizing and you've turned off the heat, drop the lids into the hot water the jars are in. You can leave the jars and lids soaking in the hot water for up to an hour while you make your recipe.

When I first learned this, I thought, "I'll just always process for 10 minutes or more and never have to sterilize!" But some recipes are better with a shorter processing time. Pickles, for example, can lose their crunch if kept in the boiling water bath for longer than 5 minutes. So with some recipes, it's worth taking the time to sterilize the jars in order to be able to go with a shorter processing time.

CANNING DON'TS

There is quite a bit of erroneous information out there about canning and also about sterilizing canning jars. Remember that canning equipment and methods like those we use today were not invented until the nineteenth century. A lot of the misinformation comes from the nineteenth and twentieth centuries, when people assumed this new technique of canning must be similar to the fermenting and other forms of food preservation that they'd used previously, or when they incorrectly assumed that the vacuum seal created by the canning process was solely responsible for safely preserving the food.

An additional source of potentially dangerous canning advice comes from a library's worth of semiaccurate food preservation information from the 1960s and '70s "back to the land" movement. With all due respect to my parents' generation, "semiaccurate" is not accurate enough when it comes to food safety.

Here are some of the most common potentially dangerous "techniques" still being advocated. Please do not use any of these methods. Why risk it? The ways to preserve food explained in this book are safer and just as easy.

DO NOT use your oven or your dishwasher to "sterilize" canning jars.

DO NOT skip the boiling water bath or pressure canner processing for canning foods and turn jars upside down for a few minutes instead, before setting them upright.

DO NOT pour melted paraffin wax over hot food and consider it sealed. First of all, parafin is a petroleum product, and not only are we trying to reduce our dependence on petroleum products, but there are lots of health alerts about having them in direct contact with our food. Secondly, any bubble or air tunnel in the wax could create an imperfect seal, resulting in mold or food that doesn't keep as long as expected.

Gear and Ingredients

Pickling, like any other kind of food preparation, can either be satisfying and fun or very frustrating. This depends, in large part, on the ingredients and equipment you start out with. You don't need to spend a lot of money or time tracking down the best jars or the fanciest baby vegetables, but a basic understanding of what makes the job easier and the end result tastier is important. With these suggestions, you will be all set to enjoy making pickles as much as you love eating them.

GEAR

Gear for pickling can be as simple as a few glass jars and a refrigerator, or all tricked out with canning gear, special fermentation crocks, and personalized mail order labels. Here is the gear I use most often when I'm making pickles.

The Essentials

These are the non-negotiable must-haves. With these, you are good to go on both fermented and refrigerator pickles. For canning, you'll need a few more items, but not many.

Jars: Mason jars are attractive in a quaint way and also very useful, but don't assume you need them for your pickles. Specialized lids that can form a vacuum seal (like the two-piece lids most Mason jars come with) are only necessary for canning. For refrigerator pickles and fermented pickles, you can use almost any jar, with a few caveats.

Glass Jars: While I just mentioned that for refrigerator pickles and fermented pickles that will *not* be canned, there is no need to use canning jars, there is also no reason not to use them. I regularly save jars from store-bought foods to reuse as containers for such pickles. Note that I specified *glass*: I am not a fan of using plastic for pickles, because it tends to absorb the brine flavors and get funky (and besides, we should be moving away from using plastic in general). I don't recommend metal, either, because the acidity of both vinegar-based and fermented pickles causes metal to corrode.

Many of the recipes in this book call for pouring boiling hot pickling liquid over the other ingredients in the jars, or for ladling all of the ingredients into the jar hot (as with most chutney and relish recipes). If that is the case with the recipe you intend to make, and if you are not using canning jars, be sure that the jars you are using are heatproof.

Canning Jars: Mason jars and other brands of canning jars were originally meant to be used in canning (although nowadays they serve many other uses as well). The special technology of canning jar lids, capable of surviving high heat and creating a vacuum seal, is essential for any pickle recipes that you want to

store at room temperature for a long time. But the heat resistance of canning jars is useful even if you don't plan to seal the jars, because, as mentioned above, the pickling liquid of many refrigerator pickles is piping hot when poured into the jars.

Nonreactive Pots and Mixing Bowls: Aluminum, copper, and non-enameled cast irons can cause fruits and vegetables to lose their bright colors and to darken. Stick to stainless steel, glass (or Pyrex), or enameled cast iron. You can use food-grade plastic for mixing bowls or short brining times (as when vegetables are salted for a few hours before pickling). However, I don't recommend plastic for long-term storage. In addition to health concerns about substances that plastics can leach into food, the plastic itself tends to absorb odors and then re-emit them into any future pickles. For example, I dare you to reuse a plastic container that held kimchi for any other recipe.

Chef's Knife: Arguably the only knife you really *need*, this is a large knife that you will use in almost every pickling project (or any other kind of kitchen project). It is absolutely worth the expense to get a high-quality one. Be sure to keep it sharp: you are more likely to cut yourself accidently with a dull knife that doesn't slice consistently than with a sharp one.

Paring Knife: Useful for small precision cuts, especially in recipes that call for piercing the food with the tip of a knife to let the pickling brine in. Also essential for peeling thick-skinned vegetables such as kohlrabi and celeriac.

Measuring Cups and Spoons: Unless I'm following a recipe, I rarely pull out these measuring tools when I cook a meal, preferring to improvise and to rely on experience and instinct. But safe food preservation is a whole different ball game. Especially when making the vinegar pickles in this book, it is important to measure properly, so that you are certain of the acidity of your final product.

Ladle: You could try to get that boiling hot pickling liquid from the large pot to the small jar without a ladle, but why would you?

Colander: This bowl with holes is not just for rinsing off fruits and vegetables. It is also an essential tool for when you need to drain vegetables after the preliminary brining called for in several of the recipes.

Fine-Mesh Sieve: Serves the same function as a colander when you are straining tiny ingredients, such as seeds, that a colander couldn't catch.

Vegetable Peeler: Although technically you could use a paring knife to peel carrots, turnips, etc., a vegetable peeler makes the job so much easier that I consider it essential.

Essential Gear for Boiling Water Bath Canning

Deep Pot: It is not necessary to purchase a special canner for boiling water bath canning, but the one you use must be deep enough. For boiling water bath canning, the jars of pickles must be fully immersed with at least 1 to 2 inches of water above the lids.

Soup stock pots work well because of their depth. For small jars (½ or ¼ pint), you can use one of those pasta pots that comes with a built-in rack.

Round Rack or Alternative: This goes inside the pot, so that the glass canning jars are not bouncing on its bottom, which could cause them to crack. Pressure canners come with fitted round racks, but because you don't actually need a pressure canner for any of the recipes in this book, you may want to improvise an alternative.

A round cake rack works well; so does a trivet, if it is large enough to cover all or most of the bottom of the pot.

If you have neither of these, another option is to put a dishcloth inside the pot before you load in the jars and water. If you only have one or two jars to can, use "dummy" jars to arrive at a full load. These are simply canning jars with water in them. They keep the dishcloth in place. Otherwise, the dishcloth floats up during processing and knocks over your isolated one or two jars of pickles.

Non-Essential but Super Helpful

Canning Funnel: I almost put this in the essentials, it is so useful. This is a wide-mouthed funnel that makes it easy to pour brine over ingredients in jars. It comes in handy for non-food preservation tasks, too, such as transferring bulk grains, seeds, etc. to jars.

Jar Lifter: This tool makes it easy to move hot jars into and out of the canner, and to carry them to their cooling-off location. You will be especially grateful to have one of these when you need to remove entirely submerged jars from the steaming water of a boiling water bath. Although you can get by with a long-handled pair of tongs for that task, there's much less danger of slippage (and dropping the hot jar) with the jar lifter.

Slotted Spoon: Makes it easy to lift solid ingredients out of the pickling liquid to transfer them to jars. The reason many pickle recipes call for doing this first—before pouring in the pickling liquid—is that you can pack more food into the jar that way.

Ceramic Crock: You don't need one of these in order to successfully ferment pickles, but they are useful if you want to make batches that are larger than a single quart.

Crocks are ceramic cylinders, taller than they are wide. They may be as simple as a vessel and lid or slightly more complicated. Fancier models include

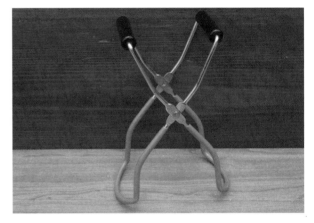

fitted weights and rims that form moats of water around the lid. This water ring seals out mold and other potentially harmful micro-organisms while allowing the gases produced by fermentation to escape. See "Useful Resources," page 256.

Weight to Fit Inside Crock: If you are making a large batch of a ferment and you don't have a crock that came with a custom-fit weight, then you will need to make one. Its purpose is to keep the solid food submerged beneath the liquid brine. No need to spend money or go high tech with this: a plate that fits inside the crock, weighted with a closed jar that is filled with water, works fine.

Many fermentation practitioners recommend using a sealed plastic bag filled with brine as a weight. The reason brine is used instead of water is as a precaution in case the bag leaks—plain water would dilute the brine. This method certainly works, but I am not a fan because the plastic is in direct contact with the food.

pH Meter: If you want to start experimenting with your own canning recipes, this is the tool that will let you know whether what you have made is acidic enough to be safely canned in a boiling water bath, or if it must be sent straight to the refrigerator (or pressure-canned, but that is outside the scope of this book).

The best pH meters are those that use an electrode. The electrode is immersed in the food and then gives you an accurate digital readout of the pH of your recipe. Food with a pH of 4.6 or lower can go into a boiling water bath (page 28).

See "Useful Resources," page 256, for places where you can get pH meters.

Acid Titration Kit: Winemakers use these inexpensive kits to test the acidity of their wines. You can use the same kit, but with different instructions, to test the acetic acid content of homemade vinegar. This will let you know whether or not it is safe to use your homemade vinegar in a pickle recipe, rather than a commercially sold vinegar. Acid titration kits are available online (see "Useful Resources," page 256).

INGREDIENTS

If you want to make pickles with vibrant colors, flavors, and textures that will make you and your guests grin, it is imperative that you begin with the right ingredients. No recipe, no matter how fabulous, can compensate for second-rate ingredients. Here is what you need to know about the ingredients that make the difference between a so-so pickle and a fantastic one.

Water

Water may seem like such a basic ingredient that there is no need to discuss it, but with pickling, the type of water you use is crucial.

For fermented pickles such as the Probiotic Fermented Radish Pickles on page 78, it is essential to use only filtered or non-chlorinated water. Chlorine and other chemicals commonly added to municipal tap water are there to kill bacteria. At the same time that they destroy potentially dangerous bacteria, these chemicals also kill the healthy, probiotic bacteria a good ferment depends upon.

For vinegar-based pickles, the type of water is less essential to the safe preservation of the food. That is because, instead of the acidity created by live fermentation, it is the acidity of the vinegar itself that kills off bacteria and mold in such recipes. However, even with vinegar-based pickles, hard water (water with a high mineral content) may cause discoloration and an "off" taste, even though the pickles are safely preserved.

If you live in a hard water area, you may want to consider softening the water you use in both fermented and vinegar-based pickles. This can be done by first boiling the water, then transferring it to a heatproof jug or bottle. A mineral sediment will form on the bottom. Pour off the water above the sediment into a second jug.

Vinegar

Vinegar preserves pickles by creating an environment that is too acidic for harmful bacteria to survive. Although a type of fermentation is required to create the vinegar itself, the ingredients in pickles that are preserved with vinegar are not considered ferments. There are four kinds of vinegar pickling.

Refrigerator pickles, so named because they are stored in the chilly environment of your refrigerator, require very little vinegar to safely preserve them. The advantage is that the lower amount of vinegar in the pickling liquid makes for a lighter, more refreshing taste and a crunchier texture than you get with other types of pickles. And you have the option of storing this kind of pickle in the freezer instead of the refrigerator, if that's where you have more storage space. The downside is that such recipes are not acidic enough to be safely canned in a boiling water bath for long-term storage at room temperature.

Canned vinegar pickles require more vinegar and have a more piercing acidity. That is a plus for recipes such as cornichons and spicy pickled carrots, but usually more than most people want in, for example, a classic dill cucumber pickle. With canned vinegar pickles, it is the acidity of the ingredients, even more than the heat and vacuum seal created by the boiling water bath, that safely preserves the food.

To be canned in a boiling water bath and stored in sealed jars at room temperature, vinegar-based pickles must have a pH of 4.6 or less. This is the second type of vinegar pickle, and it requires much more vinegar than do refrigerator pickle recipes. Want to know if your pickle is acidic enough for canning? You can buy pH meters that will tell you precisely how acidic your recipe is (see "Useful Resources," page 256). Or you can follow this rule: always start out with a vinegar that contains at least 4.5 percent acetic acid (a commercial brand will have the acetic acid percentage on the label), and never dilute the vinegar with more than an equal amount of water. If pickles made with 50-50 vinegar and water are too sour for you, try refrigerator pickles, sweet and sour pickles, or lacto-fermented pickles. (The recipes in this book will only include canning instructions when the pickle is acidic enough for boiling water bath canning.)

The third type of vinegar pickle is the kind that has enough vinegar acidity for safe boiling water bath canning but buffers the sharp flavor with sweetness from sugar or honey. Sweet and sour pickle recipes include bread 'n' butter pickles, hot dog–style relishes, chutneys, and ketchups. Usually there is little to no water added to these sweet and sour recipes.

The fourth kind of vinegar pickle starts out as a salt brine ferment. It then veers from the usual instructions for fermented pickles because vinegar is eventually added to kill off the healthy bacteria of the ferment. Although the probiotic health benefits of the fermentation are lost with this process, unique flavors are created. Also, the final product is more stable in texture and taste than live ferments are in storage. The Tabasco-Style Hot Sauce recipe on page 156 is an example of this two-step pickling method.

Of course, the vinegar in pickle recipes not only preserves the food but also contributes to the pickle's unique flavor profile. Apple cider vinegar, rice vinegar, white wine vinegar, and red wine vinegar are all excellent to pickle with. If you are making a particularly colorful pickle, white distilled vinegar is advantageous in that it shows off the bright colors of vegetables clearly. However, it has a faintly metallic aftertaste that I dislike. I usually opt for white wine vinegar when I want to show off the colors of the pickled food. White wine vinegar has a more rounded taste than distilled vinegar but a lighter color than apple cider vinegar.

Balsamic vinegar should be used for flavoring rather than a main preservation ingredient.

Although lacto-fermented pickles get more press than vinegar for their probiotic health benefits, it is worth noting that vinegar-based pickles may be health foods, too. According to the *Journal of Food Science*, vinegar has several therapeutic properties including reducing arterial pressure and the effects of diabetes, preventing cardiovascular illness, antioxidants, and antibacterial activity. And any sour flavor increases our enzyme-rich saliva, which helps us digest our food more effectively.

Salt

Choose the wrong salt and your pickle may darken to unattractively drab colors. Your fermented pickles could fail to ferment. Even the 48-Hour Mixed Garden Pickles (page 82) you threw together for a dinner party may have an unpleasant metallic aftertaste. Yikes.

Fortunately, such problems can be easily avoided by using the right kind of pickling salts and avoiding the wrong kinds.

SALTS THAT ARE GOOD FOR PICKLING

Non-Iodized Salts: Standard table salt has iodine as well as anti-caking agents added to it. It is *not* good for pickling because that added iodine can cause fruit and vegetable pickles to darken and lose their naturally attractive colors. Kosher salt and other non-iodized salts are better choices for pickling. Here are some non-iodized salts that are good for pickling:

- Sea salt may have tiny natural traces of iodine, but is fine to use in pickle recipes. The exception is sea salt flakes. Although they are delicious as a finishing salt, they measure so differently from granular salt that your recipes can get thrown off if you use them.
- Himalayan (naturally) pink salt is fine for pickling, but like sea salt, it can be pricy.
- There is something called "pickling salt" which you would think would be the best choice for making pickles. It has neither added iodine nor the anti-caking ingredients some brands add to their salt. Pickling salt is finely ground, so it dissolves quickly. It is fine to use, but for some reason it is also usually expensive compared to other equally good or better salts for pickling.
- Kosher salt is non-iodized and inexpensive. However, do take a moment to read the label and make sure there are no added anti-caking agents.

SALTS THAT ARE NOT GOOD FOR PICKLING

Low-Sodium or "Lite" Salts: In the case of lacto-fermented pickles such as kimchi, sodium is essential to the fermentation that safely preserves the food. Low-sodium salts may not create the environment that allows fermentation without mold and other nasties taking over.

You can safely use low-sodium salts in quick refrigerator and/or vinegar-brined pickles because it is the vinegar, not a salt-based ferment, that preserves the food. But I don't recommend it because of the chemical aftertaste such "lite" salts leave.

Iodized Salts: This is purely an aesthetic thing: iodized salts sometimes cause pickles to darken and lose their original colors.

Salt flakes: Sea salt flakes do not correspond in volume or weight to the measurements given in the recipes in this book or in any other pickling recipes I am aware of. You could probably get away with using them in ferments, but since they are so much more expensive than other sea salts, why bother?

Herbs and Spices

Not one of the recipes in this book calls for a store-bought, all-purpose mix of "pickling spices." The truth is that each recipe is different, and I believe that you will be more delighted with the results if your different kinds of pickles don't all taste as if they came from the same jar of seasoning.

That said, certain herbs and spices reappear in many pickle recipes, and combining them gives a familiar and scrumptious taste to many pickles. You'll want to have these in your pantry:

- Mustard Seeds
- Fresh Dill
- Whole Black Peppercorns
- Whole Allspice
- Whole Cloves
- Bay Leaves
- Whole Coriander Seeds
- Whole Celery Seeds
- Fresh Ginger
- Garlic

There are many other herbs and spices that can bring aroma and flavor to pickle recipes, but with these as your starter kit, you are already in good shape to make many of the pickles in this book.

If the herb called for is a leafy aromatic such as dill, or an underground plant part such as ginger rhizomes, choose the fresh ingredient over the dried whenever possible. Dried seeds (e.g. mustard) and bark (e.g. cinnamon) are more forgiving, and your pickles will be fine if you use the dried forms.

Remember that the same essential oils that give herbs and spices their fragrance give them their flavor, and that these oils disappear over time. If your bay leaves don't smell like anything when you crush them, they won't taste like anything either.

By the way I'm using *herbs* and *spices* in cook's lingo, since those are not scientific botanical terms. In kitchen speak, *herb* refers to the leaves and flowers of aromatic plants (dill, lavender, etc.) and *spices* are generally understood to be bark, rhizomes, or seeds (such as cinnamon, ginger, and fennel seeds).

Grape Leaves, Calcium Chloride, Alum, and Other Additions for Crunchy Pickles

Calcium chloride and alum are frequently sold as pickle additives that are supposed to improve, or at least preserve, the crunchiness of vegetable pickles. Unfortunately, they can also leave behind a slightly unpleasant, astringent aftertaste.

Your best bet for preventing mushy pickles is to use young, super-firm produce to begin with and slice off the flower ends of certain vegetables (see "Troubleshooting," page 249). But there are a few additions to your pickle jars that can help.

Grape vine leaves, cherry tree leaves, and oak leaves have all been used to help preserve pickle crunch. The reason they work has to do with their high tannin content. All you have to do is tuck one of these fresh leaves into the jar, along with the other ingredients. Keep in mind that each leaf will add its own subtle flavor to the final pickle. Don't be tempted to add extra leaves to your jars with the assumption that if a few tannins are good, more must be better. Beyond a certain amount, your taste buds will become too aware of the large amount of tannins as a mouth-puckering astringency.

Vegetables and Fruits

In general, smaller and younger is better for pickling. This translates to cucumbers that are small enough that few if any seeds have fully formed, and ditto for zucchini; green beans that snap easily and have no strings; radishes that are lightly peppery but not yet pungent; and pears and peaches that are just shy of their juicy, ready-to-eat-raw ripeness (firm enough to hold up during pickling, but still with fully developed flavor).

An exception to the smaller-and-younger-is-better rule is anything that is destined to be chutney, relish, ketchup, or sauce. For these vegetables, flavor is everything and a little mushiness is irrelevant. Bruised bits can be cut away and discarded. Such recipes are the perfect use-up for food that is too ripe for other types of pickling.

I am a huge fan of local, organic, and foraged food, but I want to stress that it is especially important to use organic produce if the peel or outer layer of the food will be included in your recipe. For example, if you are leaving the vibrantly green skins of cucumbers on when you make your Half-Sours (page 65), you don't want the mess of pesticides and wax that is on conventionally grown cukes mixed in with your brine.

Meat, Fish, Eggs, and Cheese

These should be as fresh as possible and from healthy animals that led a natural life (no antibiotic-treated, factory-farmed products).

Sassy Sour Pickles

Sour is the taste most people think of when they hear the word *pickle* **(even though there are also sweet pickles).** The recipes in this chapter will both live up to and surpass whatever expectations you might have when it comes to sour pickles.

The sourness in these recipes may come from using vinegar as a main ingredient, or it could be a result of lacto-fermentation (see "Understanding the Two Kinds of Pickling," page 19). Sour pickles made through fermentation, as well as those that use raw vinegar and are not heat-processed, give our bodies a boost, thanks to the good-for-us bacteria that they contain.

But even those that are made with pasteurized vinegar (most commercial vinegars are pasteurized) or that are canned in a boiling water bath (page 28) can be good for us. Just the fact that they are sour confers health benefits. This is because sour flavors trigger salivation, which improves our digestion because the digestive process begins in part with enzymes in our saliva.

My grandma used to say that eating something sour with meat and rich foods helped to "cut the grease." I can't promise it literally does that, but sour foods can indeed help make rich foods such as meat easier to digest.

Sour pickles can stand on their own as a snack or side to go with the main meal. They are also excellent when used as a seasoning ingredient (chopped and added to salads, dips, sandwiches, etc.)

Pickled Carrots with Coriander and Ginger

PREPARATION TIME: 15 minutes   OPTIONAL CANNING TIME: 10 minutes
WAIT TIME: 4 days   YIELD: Makes 1 pint

Made with a blend of several intensely flavored herbs and spices, these carrots are not "spicy" as in chile-pepper hot. They are spicy as in richly seasoned. Once the seasonings have had a few weeks to get to know each other, the combined flavor is smooth and even refreshing.

INGREDIENTS

1 pound carrots (use multi-colored carrots if you can find them)

1 to 2 garlic cloves, smashed

1-inch piece fresh ginger, cut into four chunks

4 to 6 whole black peppercorns

½ teaspoon whole mustard seeds

½ teaspoon whole coriander seeds

2 to 3 fresh sprigs cilantro (coriander) leaves

1 cup white wine vinegar

½ cup filtered or unchlorinated water

1 teaspoon kosher or other non-iodized salt

1 tablespoon honey

INSTRUCTIONS

1. Peel the carrots, slice off the stem ends, and trim the ends so that they will fit into a pint canning jar lengthwise, with 1 inch of head space above them. Cut them lengthwise into quarters.

2. Put the garlic, ginger, pepper, mustard, and coriander seeds into a clean pint canning jar. Tip the jar onto its side. Load in the carrot spears. When the jar is full enough for the carrots to stay vertical, set it upright.

3. Tuck in the cilantro (coriander leaf) sprigs. A chopstick is useful for pushing the herbs down in between the carrots.

4. Add more carrots until they are so tightly packed that you can't shove in a single carrot slice more without it breaking. The carrots will shrink slightly during canning, and you want them to be so tightly packed that even with that shrinkage, they hold one another down under the vinegar brine.

5. Put the vinegar, water, salt, and honey into a small pot, and bring them to a boil over high heat, stirring to dissolve the salt and honey.

6. Pour the hot vinegar brine over the carrots and other ingredients in the jar. Be sure that the food is completely immersed in the brine, but that there is still ½ inch of head space.

7. Wipe the rim of the jar clean. Screw on the canning lid. Store in the refrigerator for up to 3 months, or, for longer storage at room temperature, process in a boiling water bath (page 28) for 10 minutes. Adjust the canning time if you live at a high altitude. Either way, wait 4 days for the flavors to develop before tasting.

Change It Up: cauliflower, green or wax beans, cabbage, radishes, and baby turnips all work splendidly with the blend of spices in this brine.

Tip: Purple carrots will lose their color during the pickling and canning process, but a mix of white, yellow, and orange ones can be fun.

Cornichons

PREPARATION TIME: 10 minutes OPTIONAL CANNING TIME: 5 minutes
WAIT TIME: 1 week YIELD: Makes 2 half-pint jars

These are the tiny cucumber pickles that, in France, are served along with pâté, cheese, and other rich cured foods. The delightfully sharp tartness of diminutive pickles cuts through the richness of those heavier foods, cleansing your palate between bites.

The catch with cornichons is that you either need to be growing cucumbers in your own garden or know someone who grows them because it is essential that the cucumbers are no longer or wider than your pinkie finger (obviously pinkie finger–size varies from person to person: no more than 3 inches long and less than ½ inch thick is about right). If you've got a vegetable garden, or even a few pots on a fire escape, you can show off your baby cucumber crop by turning them into these cornichons.

INGREDIENTS

1 pint tiny, whole cucumbers (no thicker than ½ inch and no longer than 3 inches)

1 tablespoon kosher or other non-iodized salt

4 whole black peppercorns

8 pearl onions (optional)

2 bay leaves

¾ cup white wine vinegar

¼ cup filtered or unchlorinated water

INSTRUCTIONS

1. Wash the cucumbers. Slice a thin sliver off of the flower end (if you are not sure which end this is, slice a thin sliver off of both ends). The flower end contains enzymes that can cause the pickle to become mushy. Combine the cucumbers with the salt in a nonreactive bowl (no aluminum, copper, or non-enameled cast iron) and refrigerate overnight or for up to 24 hours.

2. Put the cucumbers in a colander and rinse them under cold water. Lay one of the half-pint jars on its side. Start laying the cucumbers in so that they will be vertical when the jar is set upright (it is easier to get them to stay neatly arranged this way than trying to hold them upright in a vertical, empty jar). Tuck in 2 of the peppercorns, 4 of the pearl onions (if using), and 1 of the bay leaves as you fill in the cucumbers. Once the jar is mostly full, you can set the jar upright and continue adding cucumbers. Keep packing them in until you simply can't wedge in even one more: they need to be this tightly packed so that they don't float up out of the vinegar brine.

3. Repeat with the second half-pint jar.

4. Combine the vinegar and water and pour over the other ingredients. Cover the jars and refrigerate immediately. Wait at least 1 week before serving.

5. For long-term storage at room temperature, use sterilized jars. Be sure to leave at least ½ inch of head space and process in a boiling water bath (page 28) for 5 minutes. Adjust the canning time if you live at a high altitude.

Dilly Beans

PREPARATION TIME: 15 minutes   OPTIONAL CANNING TIME: 10 minutes
WAIT TIME: 1 week   YIELD: Makes 1 pint

Dilly beans are one of the easiest pickles to make. You don't have to make a lot of jars of them at a time: the recipe below is for a single pint jar. They need to be processed in a boiling water bath in canning jars for long-term shelf storage, but if you have the refrigerator space, they'll last in there uncanned for at least 2 months. Canned or refrigerated, be sure to leave them alone for at least 1 week before tasting; the vinegar taste will mellow and the herbs will infuse their flavor into the vegetables during that time. Do not reduce the amount of vinegar in the recipe if you intend to can them, or they will not be safely preserved (you may, however, reduce the vinegar or increase the water if you will be treating them as refrigerator pickles instead of canning them).

INGREDIENTS

2 cups green or wax beans, washed and trimmed to fit jar lengthwise

1 sprig dill leaves or 1 dill flower head

1 bay leaf

1 sprig thyme

1 small hot pepper, fresh or dried

1 garlic clove

¾ cup wine or cider vinegar

½ cup filtered or unchlorinated water

1 teaspoon honey

½ teaspoon kosher or other non-iodized salt

Approximately 2 tablespoons olive oil

INSTRUCTIONS

1. Tightly pack beans into a clean pint canning jar. It is easier to lay the beans in lengthwise if you put the jar on its side and slide the beans in that way. Add the herbs, pepper, and garlic as you go, placing the prettier ones like the chile pepper or bay leaf between the beans and the sides of the jar.

2. Bring the vinegar, water, honey, and salt to a boil. Pour over the other ingredients.

3. Top with olive oil to cover the surface, still leaving ½ inch of head space.

4. Refrigerate immediately, or for long-term storage at room temperature, process in a boiling water bath (page 28) for 10 minutes. Adjust the canning time if you live at a high altitude.

5. Whether you opt for a refrigerator pickle or canning, wait at least 1 week for the flavors to mellow before serving.

Change It Up: This recipe works beautifully with carrot or zucchini sticks instead of the green beans. It is also good with burdock root, sweet peppers, kohlrabi, radishes, and baby turnips.

Cocktail Onions

PREPARATION TIME: 10 minutes, if using frozen pearl onions; up to 40 minutes if using fresh
OPTIONAL CANNING TIME: 10 minutes   WAIT TIME: 4 days, including 24-hour refrigeration time
YIELD: Makes 1 cup

Yep, these are *those* onions, the little ones on the toothpick in your martini. Sometimes called pickled pearl onions, they could be a real pain to make. But I'm going to share a little cheat with you that makes the process easier.

Once you've got all of the tiny onions peeled, the rest of the pickling process is a cinch. Although I'm usually a DIY gal, in this case I take a little help from the store and go with frozen pearl onions.

But if you want to use pearl onions from your garden, go for it. I've included instructions for that version, too.

Why bother making your own pickled cocktail onions when they are so easy to find at the supermarket? For one thing, the store version of pickled pearl onions is usually made with distilled white vinegar, which, as I've mentioned elsewhere, has an unpleasantly harsh taste.

Making your own with white wine vinegar produces a more rounded flavor.

And then there's your martini-loving friend's grin when you give them the gift of a bottle of their favorite booze along with your homemade cocktail onions.

INGREDIENTS

1 cup pearl onions
½ cup filtered or unchlorinated water
½ cup white wine vinegar
⅓ cup granulated sugar
1 tablespoon whole mustard seeds
½ teaspoon whole coriander seeds
8 whole black peppercorns
1 bay leaf

continued

INSTRUCTIONS

1. If starting with frozen pearl onions, thaw in the refrigerator overnight and then skip to step 2. If starting with fresh pearl onions, cut off the root and stem ends and peel them. Boil them in lightly salted water for 5 minutes. Drain them in a colander, rinse them under cold running water until no longer hot, and then drain again.

2. Combine the water, vinegar, sugar, mustard and coriander seeds, peppercorns, and bay leaf in a saucepan. Bring to a boil over medium-high heat, stirring to dissolve the sugar. Remove from the heat and pour the liquid and spices over the onions in a nonreactive pot (no aluminum, copper, or non-enameled cast iron). Cover and refrigerate for 24 hours.

3. Bring the onions and pickling liquid back to a boil over medium-high heat. Remove from the heat. Use a slotted spoon to transfer the onions to a clean, heat-proof jar (it is not necessary to sterilize the jar for this recipe). Pour the hot pickling liquid over the onions. Press down on the onions with the back of a spoon to release any air bubbles. If you will be canning the pickled onions, make sure there is at least ½ inch of head space between the surface of the liquid and the rim of the jar. Screw on the lid.

4. You can refrigerate the cocktail onions as is. For long-term storage at room temperature, process them in a boiling water bath (page 28) for 10 minutes. Adjust the canning time if you live at a high altitude. Wait at least 3 days before serving.

Change It Up: You can use sustainably harvested ramps (wild leeks a.k.a. Allium tricoccum*) instead of pearl onions. You can also use the white bases of scallions.*

Giardinera
(Italian-Style Garden Pickles)

PREPARATION TIME: 20 minutes   OPTIONAL CANNING TIME: 10 minutes

WAIT TIME: 1 week   YIELD: Makes 2½ pints

You can use other combinations of vegetables for this pickle than those I've listed in the ingredients. The whole idea is to use what is in season in your garden or at the farmers' market. (But leave out beets, unless you want the entire jar of pickles to be bright magenta).

This Italian-style pickle makes a lovely and easy antipasto dish. I like to drain the giardinera in a colander and then toss it with a good quality extra virgin olive oil before serving. You can save the pickling liquid for another use. (See "6 Ways to Use Pickle Juice" on page 15.)

INGREDIENTS

½ pound onion

½ pound carrot

½ pound bell pepper

½ pound cauliflower

½ pound celery

2 tablespoons kosher or other non-iodized salt

¼ cup granulated sugar OR 3 tablespoons honey

1 tablespoon whole mustard seeds

¼ teaspoon turmeric

6 whole allspice

1½ cups cider or white wine vinegar

1 cup filtered or unchlorinated water

3 to 5 sprigs fresh dill

1 small handful celery leaves

3 small hot chile peppers (optional)

continued

INSTRUCTIONS

1. Peel the onion and carrot. Remove the pith and seeds from the bell pepper. Remove the core and leaves from the cauliflower. Cut the cauliflower into florets and the bell pepper and onion into strips. I like to cut the carrot and celery in ½-inch-thick slices on a diagonal.

2. Bring a small pot of water to a boil. Drop in the celery for 1 minute. Drain, and immediately run under cold water or transfer to a bowl of ice water. Drain again. You can skip this step, but it helps keep the celery bright green even after it is pickled.

3. Combine all of the vegetables with the salt and let sit for at least 1 hour but as long as 4 hours.

4. Rinse the vegetables and drain them in a colander.

5. Combine the sugar or honey, mustard seeds, turmeric, allspice, vinegar, and water in a saucepan and bring to a boil.

6. While the spiced vinegar mixture is coming to a boil, divide the dill, celery leaves, and chile peppers (if using) between two pint jars and one half-pint jar, or five half-pint jars.

7. Pack the vegetables into the jars, leaving 1 inch of head space. Pour the hot brine over the vegetables, which should be completely covered with the brine. There should still be at least ½ inch of head space between the surface of the liquid and the rims of the jars.

8. Screw on the lids and either put into the refrigerator or process in a boiling water bath (page 28) for 10 minutes. Adjust the canning time if you live at a high altitude.

9. Wait at least 1 week for the flavors to mingle and mellow before serving (longer is even better for giardinera).

Change It Up: Other vegetables that are good in giardinera include cabbage, green or wax beans, kohlrabi, chayote, and cucumber. For my foraging friends, yellow dock flower stalks and purslane stems work well here, as long as they are not more than 25 percent of the vegetables included (more than that and their mucilaginous properties take over everything else).

Hamburger Dill Pickle Chips

PREPARATION TIME: 20 minutes   OPTIONAL CANNING TIME: 10 minutes
WAIT TIME: 2 weeks, plus 6 to 8 hours initial brining time   YIELD: Makes approximately 4 pints

Yes, these are those tangy slices embedded in your hamburger bun . . . only better. And they are just as good on other sandwiches and wraps. These pickles love ketchup, mustard, and mayonnaise, so if your meal is going to include any of those (even if it is not a hamburger), count these pickle chips in.

INGREDIENTS

3 tablespoons kosher or other non-iodized salt

10 cups filtered or unchlorinated water

2 pounds small cucumbers

4 to 8 sprigs fresh dill

4 to 8 garlic cloves, lightly smashed

2 teaspoons whole mustard seeds

¼ teaspoon turmeric powder (optional)

2 cups cider vinegar

INSTRUCTIONS

1. Combine 2 tablespoons of the salt and 7 cups of the water in a nonreactive bowl (no aluminum, copper, or non-enameled cast iron).

2. Cut a thin slice off of each of the ends of the cucumbers. Slice crosswise into pieces that are approximately ⅛-inch thick.

3. Put the cucumbers into the brine. Place a plate on top of them to keep them submerged. Let sit at room temperature for 6 to 8 hours.

4. Drain and rinse off the cucumbers in a colander.

5. Divide the dill, garlic cloves, and mustard seeds between four clean pint canning jars (the jars do not need to be sterilized). Use a larger amount of dill and garlic if you want a strongly seasoned flavor.

6. Bring the turmeric (if using), the vinegar, and the remaining salt and water to a boil in a small pot. Pour over the other ingredients in the jars. Press down on the cucumbers with your clean fingers or the back of a clean spoon to release any air bubbles. The cucumbers should be fully immersed in the liquid, and there should be at least ½ inch of

head space between the surface of the liquid and the rim of the jar. Wipe the rims of the jars dry with a paper towel or clean cloth.

7. Screw on the lids. Now you have a choice: You could simply put the jars into the refrigerator, or, for long-term storage at room temperature, process them in a boiling water bath (page 28) for 10 minutes. Adjust the canning time if you live at a high altitude.

8. Whether you opted for immediate refrigeration or canning, wait at least 2 weeks before serving.

Kohlrabi Ferment with Tomatoes and Scallions

PREPARATION TIME: 10 minutes
WAIT TIME: 2 weeks, including initial days of fermentation at room temperature   YIELD: Makes 2 pints

When the farmer for our Community Supported Agriculture (CSA) share used to send kohlrabi our way, it always generated a flurry of "How the heck do we prepare that?!" messages. Common elsewhere in the world, this cousin of broccoli and cauliflower is just starting to catch on in the United States. Useful both raw and cooked, kohlrabi deserves to be welcomed into our kitchens.

This probiotic pickle infuses kohlrabi with the Mediterranean-style combination of sundried tomatoes and oregano. Served with a little good olive oil, early in its fermentation (no older than 3 weeks), the sourness is light enough that you can treat it more like a salad than a pickle.

As it continues to age, the flavors will intensify, in a good way, but then it will be better served as an accompaniment to other dishes rather than as its own course.

INGREDIENTS

1 pound kohlrabi

¼ cup sundried tomatoes

12 scallions

8 whole black peppercorns

2 small sprigs fresh oregano OR 1 teaspoon dried oregano

1 tablespoon kosher or other non-iodized salt

1 pint filtered or unchlorinated water

INSTRUCTIONS

1. Slice the ends off of the kohlrabis and remove the tough outer layer. Cut them into ½-inch-thick sticks.

2. Cut the sundried tomatoes into approximately ¼-inch-thick strips. If they are crispy-dried rather than leathery, rehydrate them first by soaking them in boiling hot water for 20 minutes (save the soaking water to replace part of the water in the brine—it will add a big flavor boost).

3. Cut off the root ends of the scallions and any larger, tougher green parts, but do leave some of the tender green parts attached to the white parts. Trim so that when standing up, the scallions are slightly less than the height of the jars you will be making the pickles in.

4. Divide the peppercorns between two clean pint jars. Load the kohlrabi sticks, tomato slivers, trimmed scallions, and oregano sprigs into the jars. Pack them in tightly.

5. Dissolve the salt in the water (heed the warning to use only filtered or non-chlorinated water, or the fermentation you are counting on may never start). Pour the brine over the other ingredients. Hopefully, they are packed in tightly enough to hold themselves under the brine. If any of the vegetables float up out of the liquid, tuck a piece of a cabbage or kale leaf over to hold them under the brine (or a kohlrabi leaf if you've got one big enough to cover the other ingredients in the jar).

6. Loosely secure the lids. Place the jars on plates or a tray to catch any overflow from the fermentation once it gets underway. Leave at room temperature for 3 to 5 days. Open the jars daily to check for signs of fermentation: You should see some bubbles froth up on the surface of the liquid (especially immediately after you press down on the vegetables—and the leaf covering them—with the back of a spoon). The pickle will start to develop the characteristic sour-but-clean taste and smell of a healthy lacto-fermented food.

7. Transfer the kohlrabi pickle to the refrigerator or other cold but not freezing environment. At this stage, you no longer need the plates or tray under the jar, and you can go ahead and fully close the lids. Wait at least an additional 10 days before serving.

8. To serve, drain (reserve the liquid for another use) and toss with a good-quality extra virgin olive oil.

Change It Up: Use turnips or peeled broccoli stems instead of the kohlrabi.

Tip: Do not try to peel the kohlrabi with a vegetable peeler. The fibrous outer layer is too thick to be removed that way. Instead, use a paring knife, and resign yourself to losing a substantial portion of each kohlrabi.

Nasturtium "Capers"

PREPARATION TIME: 10 minutes, plus the time it takes to gather the nasturtium pods

OPTIONAL CANNING TIME: 10 minutes   WAIT TIME: 2 weeks   YIELD: Makes 1 cup

If you grow nasturtiums in your garden, you may already know that the colorful flowers and round leaves are edible and an excellent salad addition. But you may not know that the still-green seedpods are also edible, and they make an excellent caper-like pickle.

Although true capers are made from the Mediterranean plant *Capparis spinosa*, these nasturtium buds have a similar look, texture, and burst of tangy flavor. Their flavor is different from that of *Capparis* capers, but equally good. Nasturtium has a bit of a mustard-y bite that gives these pickled bites a lot of taste layers for such a small morsel.

Use nasturtium bud "capers" in any recipe that calls for regular capers. They are great in tuna salad, on pasta or pizza (try them instead of olives), or mashed with good-quality extra virgin olive oil as a piquant spread for crackers or toast points.

INGREDIENTS

1 cup green nasturtium pods

1 large garlic clove, lightly crushed

½ cup cider vinegar

¼ cup filtered or unchlorinated water

1½ teaspoons kosher or non-iodized salt

4 whole black peppercorns

1 bay leaf

INSTRUCTIONS

1. Be sure to use only green, immature nasturtium pods that are still tender enough to pierce with a fingernail. Put them together with the garlic into a clean glass jar.

2. Put the cider vinegar, water, salt, peppercorns, and the bay leaf into a small pot and bring to a boil over high heat. Pour over the nasturtium pods, leaving ½ inch of head space if you will be canning the jar (for a refrigerator pickle version, it's fine to fill the jar all the way, but be sure the liquid is not actually touching the lid).

3. Cover and either store in the refrigerator or screw on a canning lid and process in a boiling water bath (page 28) for 10 minutes. Adjust the canning time if you live at a high altitude. Either way, wait at least 2 weeks for the flavor to develop before tasting.

Change It Up: You can make something similar by using this recipe with sow thistle and/or dandelion buds.

Pickled Mushrooms

PREPARATION TIME: 30 minutes   OPTIONAL CANNING TIME: 20 minutes
WAIT TIME: 1 month   YIELD: Makes approximately 2 pints

These richly seasoned mushrooms are good enough to eat straight out of the jar, but save a few to slice and serve on pizza, add to an antipasto plate, or use as a vodka chaser.

This recipe elevates even commercially grown supermarket button mushrooms to a higher level. But if you really want to wake up your taste buds, try making the recipe with a more assertively flavored mushroom, such as shiitake or maitake.

INGREDIENTS

2 pounds fresh mushrooms

2½ cups white wine vinegar

1½ cups filtered or unchlorinated water

¼ cup dry white wine

3 tablespoons kosher or other non-iodized salt

¼ cup diced onion

4 garlic cloves

2 to 4 bay leaves

2 teaspoons whole black peppercorns

1 teaspoon whole mustard seeds

½ teaspoon whole celery seeds

¼ teaspoon red pepper flakes (optional)

INSTRUCTIONS

1. If using cap and stem mushrooms such as super-market button mushrooms, trim off the stem ends. Leave small mushrooms whole. Cut mushrooms larger than 1 inch in halves, quarters, or thick slices (the size of the pieces will ultimately determine how many jars you need). Wash the mushrooms in cool water (ignore everything you've been told about never washing mushrooms in water. I promise they will not absorb the water).

2. Combine the vinegar, water, white wine, and salt in a large pot. Bring to a boil over high heat, stirring to dissolve the salt. Add the mushrooms and return the liquid to a boil. Reduce the heat and simmer for 10 minutes.

3. Divide the onion, garlic, bay leaves, and spices between two pint jars or four half-pint jars. Use a slotted spoon to transfer the mushrooms to the jars, leaving approximately 1 inch of head space. Pack the mushrooms down lightly.

4. Pour the hot brine over the mushrooms (save any leftover brine for your next batch of pickled mushrooms). The mushrooms should be completely immersed in the brine, and there should be ½ inch of head space between the surface of the liquid and the rims of the jars.

5. Transfer to the refrigerator or another cold, but not freezing, place. For long-term storage at room temperature, wipe the rims of the jars dry with a paper towel or clean cloth. Affix the canning lids, and process in a boiling water bath (page 28) for 20 minutes. Adjust the canning time if you live at a high altitude. It is not necessary to sterilize the jars for this recipe.

6. Whether you opted for the refrigerator pickle or canning, wait at least 1 month before serving. The difference between the flavor after 1 month and the flavor after just 1 week is significant. Patience.

Refrigerator Pickles

Some of my favorite pickles are refrigerator pickles, because they have a lighter flavor than canned pickles and usually keep more of their crunchiness.

Refrigerator pickles are safely preserved through a combination of the acidity of the pickling liquid and the cool storage temperature of your refrigerator. The reason their flavor is less pungent than that of canned pickles is that they don't contain as much vinegar (but that low vinegar content is also why they are not acidic enough for boiling water bath canning).

Just to be clear (I don't think I can say this too many times, since it is about food safety), *any* of the pickle recipes in this book could be treated as refrigerator pickles and simply transferred to cold storage without sealing the jars. But those with a higher vinegar content (and therefore a lower pH) may also be safely canned in a boiling water bath (page 28) for long-term storage in vacuum-sealed jars at room temperature.

Refrigerator pickles are super easy to make, and often even people who think they don't like pickles like these. Because they are not meant to be canned, you do not need to use special canning jars to store them. But if you give them away as gifts, do be sure to tell your lucky recipients to store them in the fridge.

I've included lacto-fermented sour pickles in this section because, as I've stated elsewhere in the book, I do not think ferments should ever be heat-processed (i.e., canned). This is not a safety issue—many ferments have a low enough pH for canning in a boiling water bath. But doing so destroys all of the probiotic health benefits that fermented pickles have. Why would you want to do that?

Note that for all of the above reasons, there are no optional canning times included in this section as there are elsewhere in the book.

Freezer pickles are simply refrigerator pickles that got moved to the freezer. You can do this with any refrigerator pickle, so long as you remember two things: 1. You need to let the pickles steep in the pickling liquid in the refrigerator for at least 2 days before you move them to the freezer. If you put them into the freezer on the same day that you make them, the flavors of the pickling liquid never fully penetrate the solid ingredients. 2. Remember to take the pickles out to thaw in the refrigerator the night before you plan to serve them.

Half-Sours

PREPARATION TIME: 10 minutes   WAIT TIME: 1 week, including 3 days' initial brining time
YIELD: Makes 2 quarts

Half-sours are cucumbers cured in a brine that contains no vinegar. These are the original deli dill pickles, and they are rich in healthy probiotics (unlike the heat-processed pickles usually sold nowadays).

Kept refrigerated. For the first 6 to 8 weeks, they have a light, fresh taste and keep much of the cucumbers' original bright green color. They are called half-sours because if you wait another month or so to eat them, you will find that their flavor has become much more intensely sour (full sours).

How these pickles came to be associated with New York City delis in particular is an interesting bit of history. During the late nineteenth and early twentieth centuries, there was a wave of Eastern European Jewish immigrants who landed in New York. Fermented pickles such as these were part of the food culture that had helped make harsh winters tolerable when no fresh vegetables were available back in the old country. When they arrived in the United States, these immigrants began selling their pickles from pushcarts. Eventually the pickles became staples in delis all over the city.

Nowadays, vendors are again hawking their homemade pickles out of barrels, but this time at the greenmarkets and in trendy pickles-only stores.

continued

INGREDIENTS

12 to 15 small, firm cucumbers (Kirby is a good variety for half-sours)

1 teaspoon whole mustard seeds

½ teaspoon whole coriander seeds

12 whole black peppercorns

¼ cup kosher or other non-iodized salt

3 pints filtered or unchlorinated water

6 garlic cloves, cut in half

4 sprigs fresh dill

2 bay leaves

2 grape vine leaves or green oak leaves or pieces of horseradish leaves (optional)

INSTRUCTIONS

1. Wash the cucumbers. Cut thin slices off of each end. (It is especially important to remove the blossom end of the cucumber because it contains enzymes that can make pickles mushy.)

2. Crush the mustard and coriander seeds and the peppercorns in a mortar and pestle or with a rolling pin or a rock.

3. Dissolve the salt in the water.

4. Load the jars with the cucumbers, adding the spices and dill sprigs as you go.

5. Pour the salt brine over the cucumbers. Make sure they are completely covered by the liquid. Place the grape vine leaves, if you are using them, over the cucumbers. Use a chopstick or the handle of a spoon to tuck the leaves in around the cucumbers. The leaves keep the cucumbers from floating up out of the brine. They also help keep the pickles crunchy because of the tannins they contain.

6. Loosely cover the jars. Place on plates and leave at room temperature for 1 to 3 days, until there are signs that a successful fermentation is underway (there will be some bubbles on the surface and a clean, lightly sour smell). The plates are there to catch the overflow that often happens during fermentation.

7. Secure the lids more tightly and transfer the pickles to the refrigerator (you don't need the plates anymore). Wait at least another 4 days before enjoying your half-sours. Wait another 2 months, and instead of half-sours, you'll have full-sour pickles!

Mustard Zucchini

PREPARATION TIME: 15 minutes   WAIT TIME: 2 weeks, plus 1 hour initial salting time
YIELD: Makes 2 pints

Make these in summer, when you can get zucchini that are so young they have barely started to develop seeds yet. When made with such baby squash, the texture of these pickles is a delightful mix of crunchy and almost creamy.

INGREDIENTS

1 pound small, firm zucchini

2 tablespoons kosher or other non-iodized salt

1 teaspoon whole mustard seeds

1 teaspoon whole black peppercorns

4 whole allspice

4 garlic cloves, lightly smashed

2 whole cloves

1 pint filtered or unchlorinated water

½ cup white wine vinegar

1 tablespoon granulated sugar

1 teaspoon prepared mustard

INSTRUCTIONS

1. Wash the zucchini and slice off the ends. Cut them in half lengthwise. As I mentioned, ideally, they are young enough squash that there are hardly any seeds. If they are a bit older and seedier, use a teaspoon to scoop out the seeds. Slice the zucchini, again lengthwise, into spears about ½ inch thick.

2. Put the zucchini spears into a large bowl and toss with 1 tablespoon of the salt. Let sit for 1 hour.

3. Drain and discard the liquid the salt has drawn out of the vegetables. Rinse the spears under cold water and drain again.

4. Divide the mustard seeds, black peppercorns, allspice, garlic, and cloves between two clean pint jars.

5. Lay the jars on their sides and start to pack in the zucchini spears. Once there are enough of them to keep each other vertical, go ahead and set the jar(s) upright. Continue packing the zucchini into the jar until you can't get in even one more without breaking the glass. The zucchini will shrink a little as it sits in the pickling liquid, and you want the spears so tightly wedged in that they do not float upwards.

6. Put the water, vinegar, sugar, remaining 1 tablespoon salt, and prepared mustard into a nonreactive saucepan (no aluminum, copper , or non-enameled cast iron). Bring to a boil, stirring to dissolve the solid ingredients.

7. Pour the hot brine over the zucchini spears in the jars. Affix the lids, then leave to cool at room temperature before transferring to the refrigerator. Wait at least 2 weeks before serving.

Change It Up: You can use other summer squash instead of zucchini, but most of them have shapes that are difficult to cut into spears. Try 1-inch cubes of yellow crookneck squash or wedges of pattypan squash.

Note: "Prepared mustard" means the creamy spreadable kind that has been made with water, vinegar, wine, or another liquid, as opposed to dry mustard powder or whole mustard seeds. Dijon works well in this recipe.

The Original House Pickles

PREPARATION TIME: 10 minutes   WAIT TIME: 3 days   YIELD: Makes 1 quart

When family members stop by and ask, "Are there any pickles?" they are not talking about anything other than this infallible recipe. It doesn't matter what other types of pickles I've got on hand, these are the ones that disappear first.

If you grow your own cucumbers or have a good farmers' market near you, choose cukes no more than an inch in diameter. At that size, there is no need to peel or remove seeds. If you're working with your average supermarket monster peel, slice in half lengthwise and use a teaspoon to scoop away the seedy centers.

INGREDIENTS

1 pint water

¼ cup plus 2 tablespoons cider vinegar

1½ tablespoons coarse non-iodized salt

1 tablespoon granulated sugar

1 teaspoon whole mustard seeds

4 to 5 whole black peppercorns

3 to 4 whole allspice

2 whole spicebush berries (optional)

1½ pounds firm, small cucumbers, cut into chunks or spears or slices, at least ½ inch thick

1 small hot chile pepper (optional)

2 to 3 garlic cloves, lightly smashed

3 hefty sprigs fresh dill

INSTRUCTIONS

1. Bring the water, vinegar, salt, and sugar to a boil, stirring to dissolve the sugar and salt.

2. Put the mustard seeds, peppercorns, allspice, and spicebush (if using) into a clean quart jar. Remember that it doesn't have to be a canning jar, because this is a refrigerator pickle that will not be canned.

3. Pack the cucumber pieces into the jar, adding the chile (if using), garlic, and dill as you go. Pack as tightly as possible—you don't want the cucumber pieces to float up out of the brine.

4. Pour the hot brine over the other ingredients. The cucumbers should be completely immersed in the brine, but unlike pickles destined for canning, it is not necessary to leave much (or any) head space between the surface of the brine and the rim of the jar.

5. Affix the lid and leave the jar of your new batch of house pickles to cool for 1 hour. Transfer to the refrigerator and wait at least 3 days for the flavors to mellow before tasting. Plan on starting a new batch as soon as you start eating this one, because they will disappear that fast.

The House Pickles, Probiotic Version

PREPARATION TIME: 15 minutes   WAIT TIME: 3 days, plus 1 hour cooling time between brining and adding the vinegar   YIELD: Makes 1 quart

As fantastic as the original version of The House Pickles is, because the pickling liquid is boiled, the pickles don't carry any of the health benefits of unpasteurized, raw vinegar. Those benefits include boosts to both the immune system and the digestive system.

I wanted to find a way to make a pickle that was just as tasty as my original recipe, but also packed that active healthy bacteria punch. You're welcome.

The recipe is basically the same as for The House Pickles, with three important changes: the type of water used, the type of vinegar used, and the instructions.

INGREDIENTS

1 pint filtered or unchlorinated water

1½ tablespoons coarse non-iodized salt

1 tablespoon granulated sugar

1 teaspoon whole mustard seeds

4 to 5 whole black peppercorns

3 to 4 whole allspice

2 whole spicebush berries (optional)

1½ pounds firm, small cucumbers, cut into chunks or spears or slices, at least ½ inch thick

1 small hot chile pepper (optional)

2 to 3 garlic cloves, lightly smashed

3 hefty sprigs fresh dill

¼ cup plus 2 tablespoons live, unpasteurized cider vinegar (with "the mother")

continued

INSTRUCTIONS

1. Bring the water, salt, and sugar to a boil, stirring to dissolve the sugar and salt.

2. Put the mustard seeds, peppercorns, allspice, and spicebush (if using) into a clean quart jar (remember that it doesn't have to be a canning jar, because this is a refrigerator pickle that will not be canned).

3. Pack the cucumber pieces into the jar, adding the chile (if using), garlic, and dill as you go. Pack as tightly as possible—you don't want the cucumber pieces to float up out of the brine.

4. Pour the hot brine over the other ingredients. The cucumbers should be completely immersed in the brine.

5. Affix lid and cool to room temperature. (It's fine to "cheat" and put the jar in the fridge to speed up this step.)

6. Remove the jar's lid and strain the liquid out into another container. Return any cucumbers that poured out with the liquid back to the jar. Combine the vinegar with the cooled brine. Pour the liquid over the cucumbers in the jar. Push the cucumbers down under the pickling liquid with your clean fingers.

7. Put the lid back on and transfer to the refrigerator. Wait at least 3 days for the flavors to marry and mellow before tasting.

WHAT IS A PROBIOTIC?

According to the Merriam-Webster Dictionary, a probiotic is "a microorganism (such as lactobacillus) that when consumed (as in a food or a dietary supplement) maintains or restores beneficial bacteria to the digestive tract; also: a product or preparation that contains such microorganisms."

Fermented Green Cherry Tomatoes

PREPARATION TIME: 15 minutes   WAIT TIME: 5 weeks, including 5 to 7 days' initial fermentation at room temperature   YIELD: Makes 2 pints

Green cherry tomato pickles are a tangy treat that are delicious served with cheese or simply as an olive-like snack. This recipe has all the probiotic health benefits of lacto-fermented foods and makes great use of this end-of-the-gardening-season ingredient.

INGREDIENTS

4 cups small green cherry tomatoes

½ cup sliced onion

4 garlic cloves

2 bay leaves

2 dill flower heads (or 3 sprigs fresh dill or 1 teaspoon dried dill weed)

1 teaspoon whole mustard seeds

½ teaspoon whole celery seed

4 whole allspice

4 whole black peppercorns

1 to 2 small hot chile peppers (optional)

3 tablespoons kosher or other non-iodized salt

4 cups filtered or unchlorinated water

continued

INSTRUCTIONS

1. Wash the green cherry tomatoes. Pierce each whole tomato with the tip of a sharp paring knife once or twice. Alternatively, poke each tomato several times with a sewing needle. This step ensures that the brine penetrates the tough skins of the tomatoes.

2. Fill a clean glass quart jar with the tomatoes, adding the onion, garlic, bay leaves, dill, mustard and celery seeds, allspice and black pepper, and chile peppers as you go. It is not necessary to sterilize the jar for this recipe; just make sure that it is clean. Tuck the bay leaves and dill in between the tomatoes and the sides of the jar if you want them to show.

3. In a separate bowl or container, add the salt to the water, stirring to dissolve. Pour the liquid salt brine over the other ingredients in the jar. The green cherry tomatoes need to be completely covered by the brine, and the brine should come all the way up to the rim of the jar. Save any leftover brine (you can store it in another clean jar in the refrigerator).

4. Place the jar of green tomatoes on a small plate or saucer. Cover loosely with a canning lid. There will be some overflow (that's what the plate or saucer is for).

5. Leave the jar out at room temperature for 5 to 7 days. Take off the lid once a day and check on the progress of your ferment. It should develop a pleasant, lightly sour scent after a few days, just like a dill cucumber pickle. Use the reserved salt brine to top up the jar, should the level of the liquid dip below the top of the food.

6. After the 5 to 7 days have passed, transfer the lacto-fermented green cherry tomato pickles to the refrigerator. You don't need to keep a saucer under them at this point. The tomatoes are ready to eat once they have fermented for a week, but they will taste even more delicious if you can convince yourself to wait a full month after you move them into the refrigerator.

Change It Up: Got green tomatoes, but big ones rather than cherries? You can still use them for this probiotic pickle. Cut them into thick wedges or slices, and—important for the texture of the final product—scoop out the seeds and seed gel and compost it. (Don't worry about the seeds germinating where you spread the finished compost, as often happens when you've composted ripe tomato seeds. Since the tomatoes were green rather than ripe, the seeds aren't viable.)

Probiotic Fermented Radish Pickles

PREPARATION TIME: 15 minutes   WAIT TIME: 11 days, including 30 minutes' initial salting and 4 days' fermentation at room temperature   YIELD: Makes 1 pint

The technique for making these Asian-style pickles is similar to that of sauerkraut, but the flavor is lightly peppery and unique. They are especially good when made with daikon radishes, but any type of radish works for this recipe. Fermented radish pickles are a terrific addition to rice bowls, sandwiches, and wraps.

INGREDIENTS

3 cups thinly sliced radishes

2 teaspoons kosher or other non-iodized salt

1 to 2 thin slices fresh ginger root

1 teaspoon coriander or cilantro seeds

¼ teaspoon red pepper flakes

INSTRUCTIONS

1. Slice the radishes into thin rounds or slivers. Put them into a nonreactive bowl (no aluminum, copper, or non-enameled cast iron) and toss them with the salt. Let sit for approximately 30 minutes while the salt draws the liquid out of the radishes. The radish slices will shrink somewhat as this happens.

2. Drain the radishes in a colander, preserving the liquid.

3. Pack the salted radishes tightly into a clean pint jar, adding the seasonings as you go. Whether or not all of the radish slices fit in the jar will depend on the type of radishes you used and how much liquid came out of them.

4. Pour the radish liquid over the ingredients in the jar. Press down with the back of a spoon or your clean fingers to release any air bubbles.

5. The radish slices should be completely immersed in the liquid. If there is not enough liquid to cover them, add filtered or unchlorinated water. There is no need to add additional salt. If you do add water, press down on the radishes again with the back of

a spoon or your clean fingers to release any new air bubbles and to mix the water with the salty brine below.

6. If the radishes float up out of the liquid, put a grape leaf or a piece of a cabbage, kale, or other large, edible leaf on top of them. Use a chopstick or table knife to tuck the edges of the leaf down along the inside of the jar. The leaf should form a cap, keeping the vegetables beneath the brine.

7. Loosely affix the jar lid and place the jar on top of a small plate (the plate catches the overflow that can occur during fermentation). Leave at room temperature for 2 to 4 days. Open the jar daily to check for signs of a successful fermentation: You will see some bubbles froth up on the surface of the liquid (especially immediately after you press down on the radishes—and the leaf covering them—with the back of a spoon). The pickle will start to develop the characteristic sour-but-clean taste and smell of a healthy lacto-fermented food. Remember that temperature affects fermentation: in a cool environment, you may need to wait an extra day or so for fermentation to kick in, whereas if it's very warm, the ferment may be ready for the next step after just 2 days.

8. Once fermentation has been underway for at least a couple of days, transfer the jar of fermented radishes to the refrigerator. There is no need to keep a plate under it at this point. Wait another week for the flavor of the pickle to develop before eating it. The flavor will get increasingly sour and spicy as it

ages (remember that refrigeration slows fermentation, but does not halt it).

9. Pickled radishes will keep in the refrigerator for at least 6 months, but are tastiest if eaten within 3 months.

Change It Up: This same recipe/method works beautifully with thinly sliced turnips, chayote, fennel bulb, and carrots. Experiment with different spices (cumin seeds, allspice, and fennel seeds work well).

Magenta Pickled Turnips

PREPARATION TIME: 15 minutes   WAIT TIME: 10 days   YIELD: Makes approximately 2 pints

Don't let the shockingly bright color throw you: there is no artificial coloring in this Armenian-style pickle. The color comes naturally from the beets in the recipe.

Turnips are a too-frequently overlooked vegetable, but this pickle makes them the star of the show. Frequently served with Middle Eastern foods, including falafel and hummus, they boost the color and taste of any sandwich or salad.

INGREDIENTS

¼ cup kosher or other non-iodized salt

1 tablespoon granulated sugar

3 bay leaves

4 whole allspice

3 cups filtered or unchlorinated water

1 cup white wine vinegar

2 pounds turnips, stem ends and root tips sliced away

1 medium beet

2 garlic cloves, lightly smashed

INSTRUCTIONS

1. Put the salt, sugar, bay leaves, allspice, and one cup of the water into a small pot. Bring to a boil over medium-high heat, stirring to dissolve the salt and sugar. Remove from the heat and stir in the rest of the water and the vinegar.

2. If the turnips are very young and small, you can leave the skins on. Otherwise, go ahead and peel them with a vegetable peeler. Cut the turnips into ½-inch-thick sticks or rounds.

3. Scrub the beet clean under running water. Cut off the stem end and root tip. Slice the beet into ½-inch-thick sticks or rounds.

4. Put the turnips, beets, and garlic into a clean glass container. Pour the pickling liquid over the other ingredients. The turnips and beets should be completely immersed in the liquid. Press down on them with the back of a spoon to release any air bubbles.

5. Cover and store in the refrigerator or other cool but not freezing place for at least 10 days before serving. During that time, the turnips will take on that great pink color from the beets, and the flavors will marry pleasingly.

Change It Up: You can use this same method and recipe to make magenta-colored pickled cauliflower.

Tip: Go ahead and serve the beets as well as the pickled turnips. Whether or not to eat the pink pickled garlic is a matter of taste: I like it, but some people find it too strong.

48-Hour Mixed Garden Pickles

PREPARATION TIME: 10 minutes   WAIT TIME: 2 days, plus 4 hours initial salting time
YIELD: Makes 4 pints

These sweet and sour mixed pickles are easy to make and ready to eat just 2 days later—perfect for when you know you've got a picnic or a potluck coming up and are short on time. But like all pickles, they are also an excellent make-ahead recipe that will keep for months.

Feel free to use other vegetables besides the ones listed here; any solid vegetable that is in season in your garden or at the farmers' market will be terrific pickled this way.

This recipe makes great freezer pickles if you want to store them that way. Just remember to transfer them to the refrigerator to thaw 24 hours before you intend to serve them.

INGREDIENTS

1 pound small, firm cucumbers

½ pound green or wax beans, ends trimmed off

1 medium onion, sliced

2 bell or other large sweet peppers

1 small hot chile pepper (optional)

2 tablespoons kosher or other non-iodized salt

⅔ cup granulated sugar

1½ cups cider vinegar

1 cup filtered or unchlorinated water

4 garlic cloves, smashed

INSTRUCTIONS

1. Slice the cucumbers into ¼-inch-thick rounds. Slice the green or wax beans into approximately 1½-inch lengths. Slice the onion. Remove the stems and seeds from the bell peppers and slice into strips. Pierce the optional chile pepper with the tip of a knife.

2. Toss the vegetables with the salt in a large nonreactive bowl (no aluminum, copper, or non-enameled cast iron). Refrigerate and let sit for 4 hours.

3. In a sieve, drain off whatever liquid the salt has drawn out of the vegetables.

4. Bring the sugar, cider vinegar, and water to a boil. While you're waiting for the liquid to boil, pack the salted vegetables into four clean heatproof jars, tucking 1 garlic clove into each jar.

5. Pour the hot pickling liquid over the other ingredients. Press down on the mixture with the back of a spoon to release any air bubbles. The vegetables should be completely submerged in the pickling liquid.

6. Cover and let cool to room temperature. Transfer to the refrigerator. Wait at least 48 hours before serving. Also leave the pickles in the refrigerator for 48 hours to allow the flavors to develop before transferring to the freezer, if you plan to store them as freezer pickles.

Change It Up: Other vegetables that work well here include cauliflower, carrots, celery, kohlrabi, chayote, celeriac (celery root), purslane stems, scallions, turnips, summer squash (including zucchini), and green tomatoes.

Tip: Wide-mouth canning jars are suitable for freezer storage, but other glass jars (including other types of canning jars) could crack in the freezer. If you are going to store pickles in the freezer, transfer them to freezer-safe containers first.

Pickled Burdock Roots with Sesame

PREPARATION TIME: 25 minutes   WAIT TIME: 24 hours   YIELD: Makes approximately 2 pints

In Japan, burdock is cultivated for its carrot-shaped roots. They are called *gobo* there. Burdock roots are increasingly easy to find at farmers' markets and large health food stores. Foragers know that they are also easy to find and harvest all across North America.

The sesame in this recipe adds not only a wonderful *umami* flavor but a unique texture as well.

Although you can use other root vegetables for this recipe and still end up with something delicious, it is worth seeking out burdock if you can find it. It has an earthy, almost mushroom-y taste that is unlike any other root vegetable I know.

INGREDIENTS

1½ pounds burdock root (*gobo*)

½ cup plus 1 tablespoon rice vinegar

¼ cup sesame seeds

¼ cup soy sauce

3 tablespoons granulated sugar

1 tablespoon mirin (you can use white wine if mirin is unavailable)

1 teaspoon toasted sesame oil

½ teaspoon grated fresh ginger

INSTRUCTIONS

1. Fill a medium nonreactive pot (no aluminum, copper, or non-enameled cast iron) with water and bring to a boil over high heat. While you are waiting for the water to boil, peel the burdock roots. Either julienne them into matchsticks or slice them on the diagonal into ¼-inch-thick oval pieces.

2. Add 1 tablespoon of the rice vinegar to the boiling water. Add the sliced burdock. Return to a boil, then reduce the heat and simmer gently for 10 minutes.

3. While the burdock is cooking, toast the sesame seeds in a dry skillet for 2 minutes, stirring constantly. Use either a mortar and pestle (or a Japanese *suribach*) or an electric grinder to grind the sesame seeds. You don't want to completely pulverize them. Stop when there is a mix of finely ground seeds and partially whole ones.

4. Drain the burdock in a colander.

5. Combine the sesame seeds with the remaining ingredients to make a slurry. Put this mixture and the burdock into a nonreactive bowl (no aluminum, copper, or non-enameled cast iron). Massage the seasoning mixture into the burdock gently with your clean hands for about 1 minute. Divide the pickle between two jars, packing it down well. Refrigerate immediately.

6. Wait at least 24 hours before serving, even better after 1 week. Will keep for at least 2 months, refrigerated.

Change It Up: Use other roots such as carrot, parsnip, radish, or beet.

Tip: If the earthy flavor of burdock is intriguing but a bit too intense for you, soak the peeled and sliced roots in cold water for 20 minutes before proceeding with the recipe. This additional step lightens the taste considerably.

Grandma's Pickled Beets (Leda's Version)

PREPARATION TIME: 25 to 50 minutes, depending on the size of the beets
OPTIONAL CANNING TIME: 15 minutes   WAIT TIME: 1 hour   YIELD: Makes 1 quart

My Grandma Nea often had a jar of pickled beets in her refrigerator. I loved them even though they were in-your-nose pungent from the amount of vinegar she used. This is my version, and I hope she wouldn't mind that they are a tad gentler in flavor.

Don't restrict yourself to serving this pickle as a garnish or condiment: it is excellent as a salad served on its own.

INGREDIENTS

2 pounds beets
3 garlic cloves, lightly smashed
1 cup red wine vinegar
1 tablespoon extra virgin olive oil, optional
Salt to taste

INSTRUCTIONS

1.   Scrub the beets clean. Put them into a pot and cover with water. Bring to a boil over high heat. Reduce heat and let them continue to cook at a moderate boil. Cook until the beets can be easily pierced with a fork but are not mushy (err on the side of underdone, if you must err). This can take between 15 to 40 minutes depending on the size of the beets. Test the beets for doneness often after

continued

15 minutes and top up with boiling hot water as needed if the beets are no longer covered by the boiling water in the pot.

2. Meanwhile, put the smashed garlic cloves into a large nonreactive bowl (no aluminum, copper, or non-enameled cast iron). Pour the vinegar over the garlic and let the garlic infuse the vinegar with flavor while the beets cook.

3. As the beets finish cooking, remove them from the boiling water with a slotted spoon. Let them rest on a plate until they are cool enough to handle but still warm.

4. Put on some household (Latex) gloves if you're worried about the beets staining your hands (they will, but it goes away in a couple of hours and a few washings). Slice off the stem and root ends of the beets and compost them. Rub the skins off of the beets. Usually, they will come off quite easily, but if any bits of skin adhere, remove them with a paring knife. Very rarely it will be nearly impossible to rub the skin off. This usually happens when the beet was very recently harvested. In that case, just use a vegetable peeler for the whole beet.

5. If the beets are very small, leave them whole. Otherwise, cut them into chunks or slices (my grandma usually went for chunks).

6. Stir the beets together with the vinegar and garlic. Let sit at room temperature for 1 hour, stirring every 15 minutes.

7. The next steps depend on whether you intend to eat the beets within a week, a month, or longer. If within a week, use a slotted spoon to transfer the beets to another bowl (reserve the beet-bright vinegar for salad dressings or another use). Toss with the optional olive oil and salt. Refrigerate.

8. If within a month, sprinkle the beets with the salt and, if you wish, the oil. Use a slotted spoon to transfer the beets and garlic to a clean glass jar. Measure the vinegar the beets soaked in. For every 1 part vinegar, add 2 parts water. Pour this mixture over the beets, cover, and refrigerate. The beets need to be completely immersed in the liquid—if they are not, make additional pickling liquid of 1 part red wine vinegar and 2 parts water. Note that this is one of the main ways my recipe differs from my grandma's: she would have covered the beets with straight-up vinegar.

9. For longer-than-a-month storage at room temperature, salt the beets to taste and then transfer them with the garlic to two clean pint jars. Measure the soaking vinegar and add an equal amount, but no more, of water. Pour the liquid over the beets. They need to be completely submerged in the liquid,

with at least ½ inch of head space above them. Secure the canning lids and process in a boiling water bath (page 28) for 15 minutes. Adjust the canning time if you live at a high altitude.

Change It Up: Add a tablespoon of tarragon vinegar or other herbal vinegar to the soaking liquid. Add a sprinkling of caraway seeds or a teaspoon of minced fresh dill.

Tip: You could chop the beets into uniform pieces before boiling so that they would have identical cooking times, but I advise against it. I find the flavor is better when they've cooked with their jackets on, rather than bleeding all that beet juice out into the water. Better than chopping before boiling is to either choose beets that are approximately all the same size or check back frequently and remove the smaller ones from the water sooner than the large ones that take longer to cook.

Pickled Eggplant with Mint

PREPARATION TIME: 20 minutes   OPTIONAL CANNING TIME: 10 minutes   WAIT TIME: 2 weeks
YIELD: Makes 2 pints

The combination of mint with garlic and cumin seeds gives this pickle a wonderful Middle Eastern-style flavor. It is excellent served on its own, but it really shines when served with lamb kebabs, lentil soup, or grilled vegetables.

INGREDIENTS

1½ pounds eggplant

1½ cups red or white wine vinegar

1 tablespoon granulated sugar OR 2 teaspoons honey

1¾ teaspoons kosher or other non-iodized salt

¼ cup lightly packed chopped fresh mint leaves

2 scant tablespoons minced garlic

½ teaspoon whole cumin seeds

1 pinch freshly ground black pepper

INSTRUCTIONS

1. Cut off the ends of the eggplant and peel it. Cut into approximately ½-inch-thick cubes.

2. Put the vinegar, sugar or honey, and salt into a nonreactive pot (no aluminum, copper, or non-enameled cast iron). Bring to a boil over medium high heat, stirring frequently to dissolve the sugar or honey.

3. Add the eggplant and bring the mixture back up to a boil. Reduce the heat and simmer for 3 minutes.

4. Use a slotted spoon to remove the eggplant to a nonreactive mixing bowl. Alternatively, drain through a colander, but—important!—have a large bowl under the colander so that you can reserve the pickling liquid.

5. Toss the eggplant in the bowl with the mint, garlic, cumin seeds, and black pepper. Pack into clean heatproof jars (it is not necessary to sterilize the jars for this recipe). If you will be canning the pickles, leave about 1 inch of head space.

6. Bring the pickling liquid back to a boil. Pour it over the eggplant. Press down on the eggplant gently with the back of a spoon to release any air bubbles. The eggplant must be completely submerged under the pickling liquid.

7. Fasten the lids. Either refrigerate immediately or, for long-term storage at room temperature, process in a boiling water bath (page 28) for 10 minutes. Adjust the canning time if you live at a high altitude.

8. Whether you opted to refrigerate or to process in a boiling water bath, wait at least 2 weeks before serving your pickled eggplant. I recommend a last-minute drizzle of extra virgin olive oil.

Change It Up: You can easily turn this recipe into a mouth-wateringly good, Italian-style appetizer. In step 3, cook the eggplant in the vinegar for a full 5 minutes. Drain well. Use fresh basil instead of the mint. Leave out the cumin seeds. Throw in a few slivers of sundried tomatoes if you like. Instead of pouring the pickling liquid over the eggplant in step 6, cover the eggplant with excellent quality extra virgin olive oil. Note that this version of the recipe is not suitable for canning: store it in the refrigerator and bring it back to room temperature (so that the olive oil can reliquefy) before serving.

Tip: Choose small, young eggplants for this recipe. Those seedy, football-size supermarket eggplants will have an unpleasantly spongy texture when pickled. Young eggplants, on the other hand, will have a texture that is a combination of creamy and firm.

Indonesian-Style Pickles (*Acar Timun*)

PREPARATION TIME: 20 minutes   WAIT TIME: 4 hours   YIELD: Makes approximately 1 quart

These are more like a delicious, slightly spicy salad in a jar than like pickles. Although they will keep in the refrigerator for months, I like them best within the first 3 months, when the cucumbers still have a pleasing texture.

Usually served with grilled skewers of poultry or other meat, *Acar Timun* is also an excellent side dish with seafood or grilled vegetables.

INGREDIENTS

1 pound small, firm cucumbers (see instructions for a workaround if all you've got are big, seedy cukes)

1 large carrot, peeled

⅓ cup thinly sliced shallots OR red onion

1½ tablespoons kosher or other non-iodized salt

2 small hot chile peppers, thinly sliced

1 teaspoon whole coriander seeds

½ cup rice vinegar

½ cup filtered or unchlorinated water

3 tablespoons granulated sugar

INSTRUCTIONS

1. Remove the ends of the cucumbers and the carrot. Cut the cucumbers in half lengthwise. If the seeds are small, ignore them. With large cucumbers, scrape the seeds out with a teaspoon.

2. Julienne the cucumbers and carrot into approximately 2-inch-long, ¼-inch-thick sticks. I do mean approximately—this recipe is very forgiving.

3. Toss the cut cucumbers, carrot, and shallots together with the salt in a large bowl. Pour 2 cups of boiling water over them and let them sit for 15 minutes. Drain, and squeeze out as much liquid as you can (don't be afraid to squeeze hard). Return the mixture to the bowl and toss with the chile peppers and coriander seeds.

4. Lightly pack the veggie mixture into clean glass jars. Bring the rice vinegar, water, and sugar to a boil in a small saucepan, stirring to dissolve the sugar. Pour the hot pickling liquid over the other ingredients. Press down on the *Acar Timun* with the back of a spoon to release any air bubbles. The vegetables should be fully submerged beneath the pickling liquid. If they are not, you will need to make a little more of the vinegar, water, and sugar mixture and add it to the jar.

Change It Up: Use zucchini, radishes, or chayote instead of the cucumbers, and scallions instead of the shallots or red onions.

Fermented Sundried Tomato Pickle

PREPARATION TIME: 30 minutes, including optional 20-minute soaking time   WAIT TIME: 1 week
YIELD: Makes 1 pint

This probiotic pickle has a rich tomato taste that is heavenly on pasta, on flatbread, added to bean soup just before serving, or as a topping for lamb chops or steamed greens.

Because the dried tomatoes lack the *Lactobacillus* bacteria that are responsible for a healthy ferment (bacteria need some moisture in order to survive), you need to add some in the form of a starter culture. You can use whey from straining yogurt or the "pickle juice" from another ferment (see page 24 for instructions on making a starter culture).

If your dried tomatoes were home-dried in a dehydrator rather than "sundried," that's terrific. They will taste just as fabulous as commercially dried tomatoes when pickled this way, maybe better because the store-brand tomatoes often contain additives. The only dried tomatoes that I do *not* recommend using are ones that have already been packed in oil. It is too hard for the good gal bacteria to get through to the starches in the tomatoes if they are blocked by an oily layer.

INGREDIENTS

1¾ to 2 cups dried tomatoes

1 teaspoon dried OR 1 sprig fresh oregano

2 garlic cloves, lightly smashed

4 whole black peppercorns

1 teaspoon kosher or other non-iodized salt

1 cup filtered or unchlorinated water

2 tablespoons starter culture (page 24)

INSTRUCTIONS

1. If the tomatoes are leathery and pliable, proceed to the next step. If they are so dry that they are brittle, pour boiling water over them and let them rehydrate for 20 minutes. Use filtered or non-chlorinated water so that you can include the soaking water as part of the brine—it adds a terrific boost of flavor.

2. It's the cook's choice whether to leave the dried tomatoes whole or use kitchen shears to snip them into ribbons. Lightly pack the tomatoes into a clean glass jar, adding the oregano, garlic, and peppercorns as you go.

3. Dissolve the salt in the water. If you rehydrated the tomatoes in step 1, include the reserved soaking water as part of the cup of liquid. Stir in the starter culture.

continued

4. Pour the brine over the tomatoes and seasonings. Press down lightly on the tomatoes with the back of a spoon or your clean fingers to release any air bubbles. The tomatoes and seasonings should be completely submerged in the brine. If they float up out of it, tuck a cabbage leaf (or other large leaf) over the top of the ingredients like a little blanket. Use a chopstick or a table knife to push the edges of the "blanket" down between the tomatoes and the inner sides of the jar.

5. Cover the jar loosely and place it on a small plate or tray to catch the overflow that is typical of the first super-active stages of a ferment. Leave at room temperature for 5 to 7 days. Open the jar daily to check for signs of successful fermentation: lightly frothy bubbles that emerge when you press down on the tomatoes with the back of a spoon, and the development of the cleanly sour aroma that is typical of a healthy fermentation.

6. After a few days, there will not be any more overflow appearing on the plate or tray, and the bubbly froth will have lessened somewhat. At this stage, securely seal the lid and transfer the fermented dried tomatoes to the refrigerator or another cold but not freezing place. You do not need to keep a plate or tray underneath the jar any longer once you transfer it to the refrigerator.

Change It Up: You can use this technique to ferment any dried fruit or vegetable. Dehydrated foods are their own unique ingredients: I wouldn't say a raisin is a lesser ingredient than a fresh grape; it's just different. A fermented pickle of dried butternut squash, for example, is going to have an intriguingly different texture and taste from that of a fresh butternut squash ferment. Not better or worse, just different.

Feel free to change the seasonings, but keep the method and the salt, water, and starter culture brine the same.

Tip: Depending on whether or not you sliced the tomatoes or left them whole, you may not have quite enough brine to fully cover them. It is essential that the food be fully immersed in the brine, so if need be, mix up a bit more, using the same ratio of 1 cup filtered or non-chlorinated water + 1 teaspoon non-iodized salt + 2 tablespoons starter culture.

Pickled Avocado with Red Onion

PREPARATION TIME: 15 minutes   WAIT TIME: 24 hours   YIELD: Makes 2 pints

These pickled avocados spread on toast or a cracker are a kind of heaven. Seriously, I could eat these every day. But besides the wonderful taste and texture, this is also a great way to preserve an abundance of avocados.

Let's say you've got more avocados in your kitchen than you and your family are going to be able to eat while still good. Maybe you are about to leave on vacation, or maybe you'll be away for some other reason, but you hate to throw those avocados out. This recipe ensures they will still taste fantastic 6 weeks from now.

INGREDIENTS

4 cups 1-inch avocado chunks, from 3 to 4 medium avocadoes

1 tablespoon lime or lemon juice

¼ pound red onions

12 whole black peppercorns

6 whole allspice

2 small hot chile peppers (optional)

1 cup white wine vinegar

1 cup filtered or unchlorinated water

1 tablespoon light honey (clover or wildflower are good here)

1 tablespoon kosher or other non-iodized salt

continued

INSTRUCTIONS

1. Remove the pits of the avocados and cut out approximate 1-inch chunks. Gently stir the avocado with the citrus juice (this helps prevent the avocado from browning while you proceed with the recipe).

2. Cut the ends off of the red onions and peel them. Cut them in half and then into crescent-shape slivers.

3. Layer the avocado and red onion in two clean pint jars, adding the black peppercorns and allspice as you go. Tuck one of the chile peppers into each jar.

4. Bring the vinegar, water, honey, and salt to a boil over medium-high heat, stirring to dissolve the honey and salt.

5. Pour the pickling liquid over the avocado and onions. Press down gently with the back of a spoon to release any air bubbles and ensure that the avocados are completely immersed in the pickling liquid.

6. Secure the lids and refrigerate for at least 24 hours before serving.

Tip: For best results with this recipe, you want to use avocados that are firm (i.e. slightly under-ripe) enough to cut into cohesive 1-inch chunks. But you also want them to be ripe enough for the finished pickle to be spreadable (or at least crushable). Choose avocadoes that are very slightly soft when you squeeze them, neither rock-hard nor mushy.

Pickled Ratatouille

PREPARATION TIME: 30 to 40 minutes   WAIT TIME: 2 days   YIELD: Makes 4 pints

Pickled ratatouille is like the ultimate antipasto. It has the eggplant, zucchini, sweet peppers, basil, and garlicky goodness of traditional ratatouille, plus the zing of wine vinegar. You can serve it in little cups as an appetizer, spread it on toast, or use it as a pasta sauce.

INGREDIENTS

1 pound eggplant, stems removed and cut into 1-inch chunks

1 pound zucchini or other summer squash, stems removed and cut into 1-inch chunks

3 medium onions, thickly sliced

¼ cup extra virgin olive oil

2 large red bell or sweet roasting peppers, cut into 1-inch squares

3 large tomatoes

4 garlic cloves, minced

1 teaspoon fresh thyme leaves

2 cups red wine vinegar

¼ cup shredded fresh basil leaves

Salt and pepper to taste

INSTRUCTIONS

1. Preheat the broiler of your oven or toaster oven.

2. In a large bowl, toss the eggplant, zucchini, onions, and sweet peppers with 3 tablespoons of the extra virgin olive oil. Spread the vegetables on a baking sheet or two. Nestle in the tomatoes, whole.

3. Broil the vegetables for 5 to 10 minutes until they are starting to show some browned spots but are not burnt. Remove them from the broiler. Lift out and set aside the tomatoes to cool slightly apart from the other vegetables.

4. Heat the remaining 1 tablespoon of extra virgin olive oil in a large pot over medium-low heat. Add the minced garlic and stir for 30 seconds. Add the thyme and the broiled vegetables (except for the tomatoes) to the pot. Cook, stirring occasionally, for 5 minutes.

5. While the other vegetables are cooking, remove the stems, most of the seed gel, and as much of the skins as you can peel off easily from the tomatoes. Coarsely chop the remaining pulp and stir the tomato into the other ingredients.

6. Add the vinegar and stir for 1 minute.

7. Remove the pot from the heat and stir in the shredded basil along with salt and pepper to taste.

8. Pack the ratatouille into clean freezer containers. Be sure to leave at least 1 inch of head space, because the ingredients will expand when frozen. But don't rush to put the pickled ratatouille in the freezer. First, keep it in the refrigerator for 2 days while the flavors develop. Enjoy immediately, store in the refrigerator for up to 2 weeks, or freeze to serve later (thaw and heat through before serving).

Change It Up: Use other summer squash, cauliflower, or kohlrabi instead of the zucchini. Add a teaspoon of red pepper flakes for a spicy variation.

Polish Dill Pickles (*Ogórki Kizone*)

PREPARATION TIME: 15 minutes   WAIT TIME: 2 to 6 weeks   YIELD: Makes 1 quart

These are the pickles everybody wants to make, and which many people all too often try to create with a vinegar-based recipe, which doesn't work. They are whole cucumber pickles with a good crunch and a savory, traditional garlic and dill flavor background.

Also called *Ogórki Kizone*, they are simply a "full sour" variation of the Half-Sours on page 65. And that's not a coincidence: many of the Jewish immigrants who sold pickles off carts in New York City in the late nineteenth and early twentieth centuries were from Poland. Usually, both half-sours and some variation of these full sour dill pickles would be on offer. You can find them both for sale at the greengrocers in New York City (and around the country) today.

For these pickles to live up to their reputation, it is essential that you start out with small

(no longer than 4 inches and no wider than an inch or so), firm cucumbers. Kirby cucumbers are famously good for pickling, especially in recipes such as this, where they are left whole. But if you are growing cucumbers in your garden, any variety of cucumber will work so long as they are young enough to be completely solid (an indication that there is no large seedy zone inside, which would guarantee a mushy pickle).

INGREDIENTS

9 or 10 pickling cucumbers

3 garlic cloves, lightly smashed

2 sprigs fresh dill OR 2 fresh dill flower heads

1 tablespoon whole mustard seeds

1 fresh grape vine leaf (optional, but helps keep the cukes crunchy)

2 tablespoons kosher or other non-iodized salt

1 quart filtered or unchlorinated water

INSTRUCTIONS

1. Wash the cucumbers and remove a thin sliver from the flower end. There are enzymes at that end of the cucumber that could cause your pickles to turn mushy. If you are not sure which end is the flower end, slice a thin sliver off both ends.

2. Put all of the ingredients but the salt and water into a clean quart jar. The cucumbers need to be tightly packed into the jar. When doing this, it helps to set the jar on its side as you load in the cucumbers. Once there are enough of them wedged in to hold each other in place, turn the jar upright. To hold the cucumbers under the brine, either wedge in the last cucumber horizontally or tuck the optional grape leaf in around the top of the pickles like a blanket (use a chopstick to tuck in the edges).

3. Dissolve the salt in the water. Pour the brine over the pickles-to-be, being sure to cover the cucumbers and seasonings completely. Press down on the pickles with the back of a spoon or your clean fingers to release any air bubbles.

4. Loosely cover the jar and place it on a plate. The plate is there to catch the overflow that often occurs during the first days of an active fermentation. The lid needs to be a little loose to allow that overflow to occur and to allow the gases that build up during fermentation to escape.

5. Every day or two, open the jar and check on the pickles. If there are still signs of active fermentation, such as bubbles frothing up when you lightly press on the cucumbers, put the lid back on and let them continue to ferment. The pickles will develop the clean, sour smell of a successful fermentation. Once fermentation slows down, tightly seal the lid and transfer the pickles to a refrigerator or another cool but not freezing place. Note that sealing the lid before active fermentation has slowed can result in soft pickles.

Tip: Your Polish pickles will ferment more quickly or more slowly depending upon the temperature of the place where you put the jar. If your "room temperature" is between 70 and 75°F, they will be ready in just 2 to 3 weeks. If closer to 60°F, it could be as long as 6 weeks.

Sweet and Sour Pickles

What do bread 'n' butter pickles, papaya chutney, hot dog relish, and tomato ketchup all have in common? Take a look at the recipe ingredients—or the ingredients on a store-brand label—and you'll see a nearly identical blend of vinegar, sugar or other sweetener, and spices. The difference is mostly in texture.

Start with a sweet and sour pickle that is in slices, spears, or big chunks. Chop that up into much smaller chunks and you've got the base of a terrific chutney. Mince that chutney, and now you've got a relish. Puree the relish, and you've just made ketchup (and yes, there are other kinds of ketchup beyond the familiar tomato version).

That is the progression we'll follow in this chapter: from sweet and sour pickles in fairly large pieces (big enough that you can spear them with a fork) to chutneys to relishes to ketchups. But keep in mind that you can always reverse that trajectory. Stop your tomato ketchup recipe before you get to the step where you puree it, and you've got a great tomato chutney, for example.

All of the recipes in this chapter are suitable for boiling water bath canning (for long term storage at room temperature), or they can simply be refrigerated and eaten within 6 weeks.

Bread 'n' Butter Pickles

PREPARATION TIME: 1 hour   OPTIONAL CANNING TIME: 5 minutes   WAIT TIME: 4 days
YIELD: Makes 2½ to 3 pints

Bread 'n' butter pickles are most famously associated with the Great Depression of the 1930s, when putting food on the table was a challenge. You didn't serve these pickles with something: they *were* the thing.

But you can use these sweet and sour slices in numerous ways, including dicing them up and adding them to mayonnaise for an instant tartar sauce. Or you can serve them as their name suggests, and as they were originally eaten, on thin slices of good bread with a smear of room temperature butter underneath them. (No, you don't need to put something else on top of the pickles. They suffice.) Or you can eat them on their own—my favorite way.

INGREDIENTS

2½ pounds firm, small cucumbers

¾ pound onions, sliced thinly

1 large red bell pepper, stemmed, seeded, and finely chopped

3 tablespoons kosher or other non-iodized salt

1½ cups cider vinegar

1½ cups granulated sugar OR 1 cup honey

¾ cup filtered or unchlorinated water

1 tablespoon whole mustard seeds

1 teaspoon whole allspice

1 teaspoon whole celery seeds

INSTRUCTIONS

1. If you plan to store the pickles in sealed jars at room temperature rather than refrigerating them right away, sterilize the canning jars.

2. While the jars are sterilizing (page 28), slice the cucumbers into thin rounds. Toss the cucumber slices with the onions, bell pepper, and salt. Put the salted vegetables into a colander set in a large bowl. Let the vegetables drain for 4 hours.

3. Rinse the vegetables under cool water to remove most of the salt. Transfer them to a large pot and add the rest of the ingredients.

4. Bring the ingredients to a boil over high heat, stirring to dissolve the sugar or honey. Turn off the heat as soon as the liquid comes to a boil.

5. With a slotted spoon, transfer the vegetables to the sterilized jars (or simply clean glass jars if you plan to refrigerate rather than can the pickles). Pack them in tightly, but leave 1 inch of head space.

6. Pour the hot brine over the vegetables. You want the pickles to be completely covered by the brine, but to still have ½ inch of head space. Lightly press down on the pickles with the back of a spoon to release any air bubbles.

7. Screw on the lids and refrigerate immediately. Or, screw on the canning lids and process in a boiling water bath (page 107) for 5 minutes. Adjust the canning time if you live at a high altitude.

8. Wait 4 days before eating the pickles. They will taste even better after a week.

Tip: Bread 'n' Butter Pickles are also good stored as freezer pickles. Skip the canning step, but do store them in the refrigerator for 48 hours to allow the flavors to develop before transferring them to freezer containers and freezing them. Remember to transfer them to the refrigerator at least 24 hours before you intend to serve them.

Pickled Ginger (*Gari*)

PREPARATION TIME: 30 minutes   OPTIONAL CANNING TIME: 10 minutes
WAIT TIME: 1 week, including 8 hours' salting time   YIELD: Makes ¾ cup

If you are a sushi and sashimi fan, then you are familiar with the little pile of pickled ginger that is served alongside these dishes as a palate cleanser. Called *gari* in Japan, store-brand pickled ginger is usually a shocking pink color that comes from food coloring nowadays. What that pink is *supposed* to come from is very young ginger rhizomes, which do turn light pink when pickled. But if you can't find young, freshly harvested ginger, go ahead and make this recipe with whatever fresh ginger is available to you. Just know that if you're working with older pieces of ginger, the color of the final pickle will be light tan rather than pink.

INGREDIENTS

4 ounces fresh ginger root, peeled

1 teaspoon kosher or other non-iodized salt

2 fresh shiso leaves (optional)

½ cup rice vinegar

3 tablespoons granulated sugar

2 tablespoons filtered or unchlorinated water

INSTRUCTIONS

1. Use a vegetable peeler to scrape off thin slices of the ginger. Place the ginger slices in a bowl and massage them with the salt. The salt will start to dissolve and lose its gritty feel. Let the salted ginger slices sit at room temperature for at least 3 hours or as long as 8 hours.

2. Put the ginger in a sieve or colander and rinse it under cold water. Squeeze out as much liquid as possible, then put the ginger into a clean glass jar. Tuck the shiso leaves, if you're using them, in among the ginger pieces.

3. Put the vinegar, sugar, and water into a small pot and bring to a boil over high heat, stirring to dissolve the sugar.

4. Pour the hot liquid over the ginger. Use the back of a spoon to press out any air bubbles and make sure that the ginger slices are completely immersed in the vinegar mixture. Cover the jar and refrigerate. For longer storage at room temperature, process in a boiling water bath (page 28) for 10 minutes. Adjust the canning time if you live at a high altitude.

5. Wait at least 1 week for the flavor to develop and mellow before serving with sushi or sashimi.

Change It Up: Add a few slices of fresh turmeric root to impart a golden color to the ginger.

Pickled Red Onions

PREPARATION TIME: 1 hour   OPTIONAL CANNING TIME: 10 minutes
WAIT TIME: 24 hours, plus approximately 1 hour total cool-down time   YIELD: Makes approximately 3 cups

Gorgeous color together with an intriguing blend of sweet, savory, sour tastes and aromatic spices, plus a superb texture that manages to include both silky softness and crunch . . . what more could you ask for in a pickle?

If served on their own as a side dish, toss them with a little extra virgin olive oil. Otherwise, pickled red onions are a treat with cured meats, pâté, cheese, or simply atop small slices of a good, chewy sourdough bread.

INGREDIENTS

4 cups white wine vinegar

1½ cups granulated sugar

1 teaspoon whole black peppercorns

4 whole allspice

3 whole cloves

1 bay leaf

1 cinnamon stick

1½ pounds red onions

INSTRUCTIONS

1. Put the white wine vinegar, sugar, and spices into a nonreactive pot (no aluminum, copper, or non-enameled cast iron). This is especially important for this recipe because a reactive pot turns the red onions a weird bluish color. Bring to a simmer, stirring occasionally to dissolve the sugar.

2. In between stirs of the pickling liquid, prep the red onions. Slice off the root and top ends of the onions. Peel them. Cut crosswise into slices a little thicker than ¼ inch.

3. Add ⅓ of the sliced onions to the simmering liquid, stirring a few times, until the liquid returns to a simmer. Remove the pot from the heat. Use a slotted spoon or tongs to transfer the onions to a plate. Put the plate in the refrigerator.

4. Bring the spiced pickling liquid back to a simmer. Put in another ⅓ of the onions. Proceed as before, and once again with the final ⅓ of the onions. It may seem like a hassle to do the onions in batches like this, but you end up with much better color and texture in the final pickle than you would if you crowded the pot.

5. After the last batch of onions has come out, cool the pickling liquid (fine to use the refrigerator again to help speed this up).

6. Pack the onions into clean half-pint jars. Pour the cooled pickling liquid over the onions. Press down on the onions with the back of a spoon to release any air bubbles and to ensure the onions are completely covered by the liquid.

7. Secure the lids and refrigerate immediately. Or, for long-term storage at room temperature, be sure to leave at least ½ inch of head space between the surface of the pickling liquid and the rims of the jars. Secure canning lids and process in a boiling water bath (page 28) for 10 minutes. Adjust the canning time if you live at a high altitude.

8. Whether you opted for a refrigerator pickle or canning, wait at least 24 hours before serving your pickled red onions.

Change It Up: You can get a very similar flavor and texture but a lighter pink color by using white or yellow onions and adding a few slices of raw beet. Just add the beet slices along with the vinegar, sugar, and spices when you start the cooking process. For an even brighter color, tuck one of the beet slices into each jar before you put the lids on.

Pickled Nori (*Tsukudani*)

PREPARATION TIME: 30 minutes   WAIT TIME: 3 hours, including cool-down time at room temperature
YIELD: Makes 1½ cups

This smooth spread gives you a blend of sweet, salty, and *umami* flavors plus the high mineral content and health benefits of all sea vegetables. The flavor is intense, but in a pleasing way. *Tsukudani* is traditionally served with rice and is also good with simply steamed vegetables or seafood.

INGREDIENTS

15 nori (yakinori) sheets

½ cup soy sauce OR tamari

¼ cup rice vinegar

2 tablespoons mirin OR white wine

1½ tablespoons granulated sugar

INSTRUCTIONS

1. Put the sheets of nori into a mixing bowl and cover them with water. Let them soak for 5 minutes. Drain in a colander and then squeeze them in a clean dishtowel to get rid of most of the liquid.

2. Put the soaked nori into a nonreactive pot (no aluminum, copper, or non-enameled cast iron). Add the rest of the ingredients. Bring the nori to a boil over high heat, then immediately reduce the heat to low and simmer, stirring often, for 15 minutes. You want most but not all of the liquid to evaporate and for the nori to become a smooth paste.

3. Transfer the pickled nori to a clean heatproof jar and cover. Let cool to room temperature, then transfer to the refrigerator. Wait at least 2 hours before serving.

Change It Up: Follow the same instructions and mostly the same ingredients list but swap the nori for kombu or wakame, or use hijiki seaweed or dulse shreds. If you use the hijiki, don't cook for quite as long, maybe 10 minutes maximum. You won't end up with a silky paste as with the nori, but rather a pickled seaweed salad ready to serve as a side dish straight out of the jar.

Tip: If you've ever done homemade sushi and ended up with a few leftover sheets of nori that got soggy or stale, this is the perfect use for them. In tsukudani the shortcomings of old nori sheets vanish and only lovely flavor and high nutritional value remain. But you'll still probably need to purchase additional nori to arrive at the 15 sheets called for in the recipe.

Butternut Squash Pickles

PREPARATION TIME: 30 minutes   OPTIONAL CANNING TIME: 10 minutes
WAIT TIME: 1 week, plus 3 hours' initial salting time   YIELD: Makes 3 pints

This lightly spiced pickle with hints of cardamom and fennel is comfort food in a jar. It is excellent served on its own as a snack but also delicious with duck or sausage.

INGREDIENTS

2½ pounds butternut squash, weighed whole (you'll need more than one squash)

1 tablespoon kosher or other non-iodized salt

2½ cups cider vinegar

¾ cup granulated sugar

1 garlic clove, lightly smashed

½-inch chunk fresh ginger, cut into thin slices

½ teaspoon whole fennel seeds

6 whole black peppercorns

2 whole cloves

1 bay leaf

1 cardamom pod, crushed

INSTRUCTIONS

1. Cut the ends off the butternut squash. Cut in half lengthwise and scoop out the seeds (you can save the seeds to toast for a healthy snack). Use a knife to remove the rind.

2. Cut the prepared squash into pieces. The pieces can be long strips or small cubes, as you wish, but make sure they are approximately ¾ inch thick.

3. Toss the butternut squash with the salt and refrigerate for 3 hours. Drain the squash in a colander, rinse under cold water to remove the salt, and drain again.

4. Bring a large pot of water to a boil. Add the squash, return to a boil, then immediately pour the water and squash into a colander to drain. Once again rinse under cold water (this time to halt any further cooking from residual heat). Drain well.

5. Put the vinegar and sugar into the pot in which you blanched the squash. Now you have a choice: you can either simply put all of the spices in with the vinegar and sugar and strain them out at the end, or you can tie them up into a cheesecloth

bundle. Either way, do not leave the spices in the pickling liquid in the end, or the flavor becomes too strong over time.

6. Bring the vinegar, sugar, and spices (or spice bundle) to a boil. Reduce the heat and simmer for 5 minutes. Remove from the heat and let the spices steep for an additional 5 minutes.

7. Meanwhile, pack the butternut squash pieces into clean, heatproof jars. Remove the cheesecloth spice bundle from the liquid, or strain the liquid through a fine-mesh sieve. Pour the still hot brine over the squash in the jars. Press down on the squash with the back of a spoon to release any air bubbles and to push the squash down so that it is beneath the surface of the liquid. If you intend to can the pickle, make sure to leave at least ½ inch of head space between the surface of the pickling liquid and the rims of the jars.

8. Either refrigerate immediately, or, for long term storage at room temperature, process in a boiling water bath (page 28) for 10 minutes. Adjust the canning time if you live at a high altitude.

9. Whether you decided to refrigerate immediately or opted for canning, wait at least 1 week before serving your butternut squash pickle.

Change It Up: You can use other varieties of winter squash in this recipe instead of the butternut squash. Acorn squash, pumpkin, and kabocha are all excellent when pickled. But don't use delicata squash or other varieties, whose flesh is thinner than ¾ inch.

Tip: Do not slice the butternut squash pieces thinner than ¾ inch, or the pickle will be too soft to pick up in whole pieces. If you intend to process the squash in a boiling water bath rather than simply refrigerating it, I recommend making the pieces a full inch thick, because the canning process further softens the squash.

Chinese-Style Sweet and Sour Spicy Cabbage

PREPARATION TIME: 20 minutes   WAIT TIME: 24 hours, plus 1 hour initial salt brining time

YIELD: Makes approximately 2 pints

If you've eaten at a really good Chinese restaurant, then you have eaten this pickle. It is crunchy, both lightly sweet and sour, and may be either not at all spicy or wickedly fiery depending on the house recipe.

Leave the chile peppers out if spicy food is not your thing, or feel free to add more if you want to crank up the heat.

INGREDIENTS

2 pounds cabbage

2 large carrots

¼ cup kosher or other non-iodized salt

2 cups filtered or unchlorinated water

1 cup white wine OR rice vinegar

⅔ cup granulated sugar

4 whole Sichuan peppercorns OR 6 whole black peppercorns

2 to 3 garlic cloves, lightly crushed

2 to 4 fresh or whole dried red chile peppers OR ½ teaspoon red pepper flakes (optional)

INSTRUCTIONS

1. Cut the cabbage(s) in half lengthwise and then cut out and compost the solid cores. Save a couple of large, whole cabbage leaves for one of the final steps in the recipe. Chop or tear the rest of the leaves into 2- to 3-inch chunks. Peel the carrots and cut them into ¼-inch-thick matchsticks or rounds.

2. Put the cabbage and carrots into a large nonreactive mixing bowl (no aluminum, copper, or non-enameled cast iron). Add the salt and lightly massage the mixture with your clean hands to thoroughly combine the ingredients and to start to release the juices in the cabbage. Don't worry that it may seem like a lot of salt: it gets rinsed off before you proceed with the pickling.

3. Find a plate that fits inside the mixing bowl (resting on the cabbage mixture). Put a weight on the plate (a jar of water works well, but just be sure to have the lid fastened on so that the water doesn't spill into the bowl). Refrigerate for 1 hour. The salt will draw some liquid out of the veggies, and you will see it pooling up in the bowl under the solid ingredients.

4. While the vegetables are being salt brined, put the water, vinegar, sugar, and peppercorns into a nonreactive pot and bring them to a boil, stirring to dissolve the sugar. Remove from the heat and let cool to room temperature (if you do this step right after you put the cabbage into the refrigerator, the pickling liquid will be the perfect temperature to proceed after 1 hour).

5. Drain the cabbage and carrots in a colander. Rinse well under cool water. Roll the vegetables up in a clean dishtowel and squeeze hard to remove as much liquid as possible (you may need to do this in batches).

6. Return the vegetables to the mixing bowl and toss with the garlic and the chile peppers, if using. Lightly pack the mixture into clean glass jars. Pour the cooled pickling liquid over the cabbage and other ingredients. You can save any leftover pickling liquid in a clearly labeled jar in the refrigerator to use with future batches of pickled cabbage.

7. Press down on the pickle lightly with the back of a spoon to release any air bubbles. The vegetables need to be completely immersed in the pickling liquid. If they are floating up out of the liquid, take the whole cabbage leaves you reserved at the beginning of the recipe and place them over the other ingredients like a little blanket. Use a chopstick to tuck the edges of the leaf down around the inside of the jar. This "blanket" keeps the other ingredients submerged in the liquid.

8. Cover, refrigerate, and wait at least 24 hours before serving. Store in the refrigerator.

Change It Up: Break a star anise seed pod apart and add two of its sections to the pickling liquid. Remove them before pouring the liquid over the other ingredients because the flavor intensifies over time and becomes too strong if left in. But the 1-hour cool-down time is just enough to lightly infuse the liquid with a hint of anise flavor.

Tip: Choose round heads of cabbage (rather than Napa or some other variety) that feel solid when you squeeze them. This will give you the best texture in the finished pickle.

CHUTNEY

Chutney is originally from India, where it is called *chatni* and where it is made with many different fruits. In India, chutney can be chunky or so finely chopped that it is more like what I call a relish, or even a thin sauce. But the chutneys that have become popular around the world tend to be chunky.

Chutney is a taste bud tantalizer that, of course, goes perfectly with the many types of Indian curries, as well as samosas, pakora, and many kinds of Indian street food. But it has also been adopted into the cuisines of the Caribbean and many parts of Africa. It was famously popularized in Great Britain as Major Grey's Mango Chutney.

Chutney is a great way to preserve very ripe fruit that has a few bruises or is too soft to make into a good finger-food pickle.

Chutney has many uses besides playing a supporting role to curried main courses. Try it on soft cheeses, grilled meat, yogurt, mashed into cream cheese or bean puree as a sandwich spread, and mixed into rice or other cooked grains.

Apple Chutney

PREPARATION TIME: 35 minutes, including 25 minutes' cooking time
OPTIONAL CANNING TIME: 10 minutes   WAIT TIME: 1 week   YIELD: Makes approximately 4 pints

Of course, you can use this lovely, simple chutney in all the ways mentioned on the previous pages. But if you're feeling fancy, try apple chutney baked inside pastry dough with brie cheese, for my favorite variation of *brie en croute*. Or, on a tired night that needs some spice, put a dollop on your plate beside your chicken or rice and be grateful for the time you took to make apple chutney on some previous, perkier day.

INGREDIENTS

4 pounds apples or other fruit or vegetable (see note for best options), cored and finely chopped

2½ cups cider vinegar

2 cups light brown sugar OR 1½ cups honey

1½ cups raisins

1 organic lemon, quartered and thinly sliced (include the peel but discard the seeds)

⅓ cup finely chopped onion

1 garlic clove, minced

1 tablespoon grated fresh ginger

1 teaspoon whole coriander seeds

½ teaspoon kosher or other non-iodized salt

¼ teaspoon ground allspice

¼ teaspoon ground cinnamon

Pinch ground cloves

1 teaspoon minced fresh chile pepper OR ½ teaspoon red pepper flakes (optional)

INSTRUCTIONS

1. Put all the ingredients in a large pot over medium-high heat.

2. Boil until the fruit or vegetables are soft, about 25 minutes. The chutney is done when a spoon dragged across the bottom of the pot leaves a trail that doesn't fill in immediately. If the chutney reaches this stage before the fruit or vegetable is completely soft, add a splash of cider vinegar.

3. Chutney will keep in the refrigerator for up to 1 month. For longer storage at room temperature, can the chutney in half-pint or pint canning jars in a boiling water bath (page 28) for 10 minutes. Adjust the canning time if you live at a high altitude. Wait at least 1 week for the flavors to mellow and marry before sampling.

Change It Up: You can think of this as a master recipe for fruit chutney. Try it with fruits other than apples. Consider slightly underripe peaches, nectarines, and apricots, which will have enough backbone to still contribute a chunky texture but be ripe enough to fill the chutney with flavor.

Chunky Papaya Chutney with Rum

PREPARATION TIME: 30 minutes   OPTIONAL CANNING TIME: 15 minutes
WAIT TIME: 1 week   YIELD: Makes 2 half-pint jars

Serve this with white fish, scallops, or lobster, or just eat it straight out of the jar (it's that good). The rum is a background flavor note that doesn't knock you out but instead pairs perfectly with the papaya and seasonings. Unlike the usual papaya preserve recipes that call for using underripe fruit because it is firmer, in this case choose juicy, soft, fully ripe papaya.

INGREDIENTS

5 cups 1-inch chunks ripe papaya

½ cup raw/demerara sugar

¾ cup rice wine OR cider vinegar

2 tablespoons rum

¼ cup finely chopped onion

½ teaspoon minced garlic

1 slice fresh ginger root, approximately 2 inches long and ⅛ inch thick

½ teaspoon whole mustard seeds

¼ teaspoon whole coriander seeds

¼ to ½ teaspoon red pepper flakes

4 whole black peppercorns

INSTRUCTIONS

1. Put all of the ingredients into a nonreactive pot (no aluminum, copper, or non-enameled cast iron). Bring to a boil. Cook, stirring often, until there is still some liquid, but the trail left by a spoon swiped through the chutney does not fill in immediately.

2. Remove the slice of ginger. Pack into a clean canning jar. Process in a boiling water bath (page 28) for 15 minutes. Adjust the canning time if you live at a high altitude. Alternatively, skip the canning process and refrigerate your papaya chutney for up to 3 months.

3. Wait at least 1 week for the flavors to mellow and mingle before serving.

Fermented Pear Chutney with Ginger

PREPARATION TIME: 20 minutes

WAIT TIME: 9 days, including 2 days' initial fermentation at room temperature   YIELD: Makes 1 quart

Fermented chutney has a lighter taste than the usual cooked kind, so much so that I sometimes call it fruit salsa instead of chutney. In addition to the always excellent combination of pears and ginger, this chutney brings a dose of healthy prebiotics and probiotics to your meal. You can serve it in the usual way—as a condiment to go with other foods—but this one is also wonderful when served on its own as an unusual side dish.

Note that there is no canning time listed below, because this is a live, probiotic recipe, and why would you kill all that goodness by canning it?

INGREDIENTS

3 tablespoons cider vinegar, divided

1 quart plus ½ cup filtered or unchlorinated water

2 tablespoons honey OR agave nectar

2 tablespoons whey (optional but useful, see page 24 for how to make a whey starter culture.)

2 teaspoons kosher or other non-iodized salt

3 cups chopped pears (from about 4 large pears)

¾ teaspoon whole coriander seeds

½ cup golden raisins

¼ cup thinly sliced onion

2 tablespoons minced fresh ginger

½ teaspoon red pepper flakes

INSTRUCTIONS

1. Prepare an acidulated water bath by mixing 2 tablespoons of the cider vinegar with 1 quart of filtered or non-chlorinated water in a large bowl.

2. In a separate bowl or container, whisk together the acidulated water, honey, whey (if using), salt, and the remaining tablespoon of vinegar until the honey and salt are completely dissolved.

3. Peel the pears. Slice off the stem and bottom ends. Cut them in half lengthwise and scoop out the core where the seeds are. Cut the peeled, seeded pears into slices or slivers between ⅛ and ¼ inch thick. Drop the pieces into the bowl of acidulated water as you go to minimize browning.

4. Lightly crush the coriander seeds with a mortar and pestle.

5. Coarsely chop the raisins (you can skip this step if you like, but I think the texture of this chutney is better if you take the time to do it).

6. In a large bowl, mix together the pears, raisins, onion slices, minced ginger, coriander, and red pepper flakes. Pack the combined ingredients into a clean glass quart jar.

7. Pour the brine over the other ingredients. The brine should completely cover the pears and other ingredients: if it does not, top off with a little filtered water.

8. Press down on the chutney with the back of a spoon to release any air bubbles.

9. Put a lid on the jar, but loosely (you want the gases that develop during fermentation to be able to escape). Put a small plate under the jar to catch any overflow that may occur during fermentation.

10. Leave the jar of pear chutney out at room temperature for 2 days. During that time, take the lid off at least once a day and look for signs of fermentation, such as bubbles on the surface. You'll see these especially if you press gently on the food with the back of a spoon. But don't just *look* for signs of fermentation: also get close with your nose and sniff for that lightly sour, tangy smell that means the safe, tasty, and healthy transformation you are after is happening. But also expect that, because of the spices, your fermenting fruit chutney will be more aromatic than simpler fermented pickle recipes.

11. Once the gingered pear chutney has been actively fermenting for at least 48 hours, transfer it to the refrigerator or another cool, but not freezing, place. You won't need the plate under the jar any longer because the cold storage temperature will slow fermentation down so much that there should not be any overflow. If you put your probiotic chutney in the refrigerator, store it on the top shelf of the main compartment, which is the coolest part of the refrigerator. This will help the pears keep a pleasing texture longer. Wait at least a week more before eating the chutney.

Change It Up: Use peaches or nectarines instead of the pears. Add 2 sticks of cinnamon to the jar instead of (or in addition to) the ginger.

Tip: For the best texture in your fermented pear chutney, use fruit that is firm and slightly underripe. That is good advice for the peach or nectarine variations as well.

Mulberry Chutney

PREPARATION TIME: 20 minutes   OPTIONAL CANNING TIME: 10 minutes
WAIT TIME: 1 week   YIELD: Makes 1 pint

Mulberry trees are common in both rural and urban areas across North America. Once upon a time, they were intentionally planted for their fruit. Nowadays, people usually just curse the pavement-staining berries and leave them to stain the sidewalk. What a waste! This delicious fruit is easy to identify, tasty, and as worth including in our meals as it was in our great-grandparents' meals.

But if you don't have a mulberry tree in your neighborhood, don't fret. This recipe can also be made with dried mulberries (available at many health food stores if you don't dehydrate your own).

INGREDIENTS

2 cups fresh or rehydrated dried mulberries, or a combination of both

½ cup cider vinegar

½ cup finely chopped apple

⅓ cup honey

¼ cup finely chopped onion

¼ cup raisins

1-inch piece fresh ginger, peeled and grated

1 teaspoon red pepper flakes (optional)

1 teaspoon kosher or other non-iodized salt

¾ teaspoon ground spicebush berries OR ½ teaspoon ground allspice plus ¼ teaspoon ground pepper

¼ teaspoon ground cardamom

INSTRUCTIONS

1. Combine all of the ingredients in a pot over medium heat. Simmer, stirring frequently, until most of the liquid has evaporated or been absorbed (the track left on the bottom of the pot when you drag a wooden spoon through the chutney should not fill back in immediately).

2. Pack the mulberry chutney into a clean heat-proof jar(s). If you will be canning the chutney, leave at least ½ inch of head space between the surface of the chutney and the rim of the jar. Secure the lid(s). Refrigerate immediately or proceed to the next step.

3. For long-term storage at room temperature, process in a boiling water bath (page 28) for 10 minutes. Adjust the canning time if you live at a high altitude.

4. Whether you refrigerated the chutney immediately or chose to can it, wait at least 1 week for the flavors to develop before serving.

Change It Up: You can also make this chutney with blackberries or raspberries. The flavor will be entirely different, but still wonderful. With these berries, I recommend adding a tiny pinch of ground cloves.

Tip: Frozen mulberries (or blackberries or raspberries) will work just as well in this recipe as fresh berries.

Dried Fruit Chutney
(*Lagan Nu Achaar*)

PREPARATION TIME: 2 hours   OPTIONAL CANNING TIME: 10 minutes
WAIT TIME: 2 weeks, including 20 minutes' maceration time   YIELD: Makes approximately 5 pints

This is a Persian recipe traditionally served as part of a wedding menu. Simple to make, it enlivens everything from meat dishes to plain rice. Believe it or not, this version contains much less sugar than is called for in traditional *Lagan Nu Achaar*! It is meant to be eaten in small spoonfuls alongside spiced dishes such as curries. Although it is usually called "Persian Wedding Pickle," I think of it more as a chutney.

INGREDIENTS

1½ cups chopped dried apricots

1 cup raisins

10 dried dates, pits removed, chopped

2 pounds granulated sugar

3½ cups cider vinegar

4 pounds carrots

3½ tablespoons peeled and minced fresh ginger

1 teaspoon kosher or other non-iodized salt

1½ tablespoons garam masala

1 teaspoon red pepper flakes

INSTRUCTIONS

1. Stir the apricots, raisins, and dates together with 1 cup of the sugar and 1 cup of the vinegar. Cover and let sit at room temperature overnight.

2. Peel the carrots. Either grate them on the coarse holes of a grater or pulse them in a food processor.

3. In a large pot, cook the carrots over medium heat together with the rest of the sugar and vinegar. Stir frequently. When the carrots soften, add the ginger and salt. Continue to cook until the consistency is that of a sticky syrup.

4. Add the dried fruits along with their soaking liquid. Bring to a boil. Stir in the garam masala and red pepper flakes. The mixture should be thick enough to fall slowly off a spoon in a mass rather than pour. If it is not, boil it for a few more minutes.

5. Transfer to clean jars and store in the refrigerator or another cold but not freezing place (such as a cellar). For long-term storage at room temperature, process in a boiling water bath (page 28) for 10 minutes. Adjust the canning time if you live at a high altitude.

6. Wait at least 2 weeks for the flavors to develop before serving.

Tip: Chopping dried fruit isn't a fun task since it sticks to your knife and even a food processor can choke on it. Put a little vegetable oil on your knife or on the blades of your food processor. It makes this part of the preparation much, much easier.

RELISH

Like bread 'n' butter pickles and chutneys, relishes
are usually sweet and sour condiments that combine
full-strength vinegar with sugar or honey. The difference between the two types of condiments is in their
texture, which is that of finely chopped or minced
ingredients as opposed to bigger chunks or smooth
spreads.

Classic Hot Dog Relish

PREPARATION TIME: 40 minutes   OPTIONAL CANNING TIME: 10 minutes
WAIT TIME: 1 week, including overnight salting time   YIELD: Makes four half-pint jars

This relish is a must-have right alongside ketchup, mustard, and sauerkraut on any build-your-own-hot-dog buffet. But don't just use it on hot dogs. It is also fabulous with deviled eggs and potato salad, as well as mixed with mayonnaise for a sort of instant tartar sauce for seafood.

INGREDIENTS

4 cups finely chopped cucumbers (see Instructions)

2 large green bell pepper

2 medium to large onions

2 tablespoons kosher or other non-iodized salt

1½ teaspoons cornstarch

½ cup cider vinegar

½ teaspoon celery seed

⅛ teaspoon freshly ground nutmeg

⅛ teaspoon freshly ground black pepper

¾ cup granulated sugar OR ½ cup light honey (orange blossom or clover honey works well)

INSTRUCTIONS

1. Wash the cucumbers. Slice off the stem ends of the cucumbers. Cut the cucumbers in half lengthwise. If they are very seedy, use a small spoon to scoop out and compost or discard the seeds. Finely chop the cucumbers or pulse them a few times in a food processor. You want them to be minced but not pureed.

2. Slice off the stem of the green bell pepper. Cut them in half and remove the seeds and any white pith. Slice the ends off of the onions and peel them. Finely chop the pepper and onions or pulse them a few times in a food processor. As with the cucumbers, you want them to be minced, but not pureed into mush.

3. Combine the cucumbers, sweet pepper, and onions in a large bowl. Add the salt and mix well. Don't worry if it seems like a lot of salt—you'll be rinsing most of it off in the next step. The salt will draw water out of the vegetables, which will result in better taste and texture in the finished relish.

continued

4. Cover the bowl of salted vegetables and leave it in the refrigerator overnight or for 8 to 12 hours.

5. Put the vegetables into a finely meshed sieve and let them drain for a couple of minutes. Rinse them under cold water and then let them drain again for another minute or two. Press on the vegetables with the back of a wood spoon or your clean hands to remove as much liquid as possible.

6. In a large pot, whisk the cornstarch into the cider vinegar. Add the spices and sugar or honey, and bring the mixture to a boil over medium heat, stirring to dissolve the sugar or honey.

7. Once the spiced vinegar syrup is boiling, add the minced vegetables. Bring the mixture back to a boil, then reduce the heat and simmer, stirring occasionally, for 10 minutes.

8. Spoon the relish into clean, hot canning jars. Press down on the relish with the back of a spoon or your clean fingers to release any air bubbles.

   Leave ½ inch of head space. Screw on the canning lids and process the relish in a boiling water bath (page 28) for 10 minutes. Adjust the canning time if you live at a high altitude. Once canned in a boiling water bath, the relish will keep inside the sealed jars at room temperature for at least a year. Once opened, the relish will keep in the refrigerator for up to 3 months.

9. Wait at least a week for the flavors to mingle and develop before serving the relish.

Change It Up: Use zucchini or green tomatoes instead of the cucumber. Use red, orange, or yellow sweet peppers instead of the green peppers for a less traditional and more lively color.

Piccalilli

PREPARATION TIME: 20 minutes   OPTIONAL CANNING TIME: 10 minutes
WAIT TIME: 1 month, including overnight initial salting time   YIELD: Makes 3 pints

Piccalilli is an old-fashioned relish served in the UK along with "a ploughman's lunch." Traditionally, this included a hunk of bread, a slice or two of onion, some sausage, and maybe a piece of cheese. Contemporary restaurants have built the Ploughman's Lunch into a showcase for charcuterie, but even those upscale eateries know it wouldn't be the real deal without a colorful, tangy heap of piccalilli.

Want to skip the full ploughman's lunch and keep it simple? Scoop some piccalilli onto an open-face cheese sandwich.

INGREDIENTS

1 pound cauliflower

½ pound green beans

1 large onion

1 large carrot, peeled

3 tablespoons kosher or other non-iodized salt

2 tablespoons corn starch

1 tablespoon whole mustard seeds

1 teaspoon turmeric

1 teaspoon mustard powder

¾ teaspoon ground cumin

¾ teaspoon ground coriander

4 whole allspice

2½ cups cider vinegar

⅓ cup granulated sugar

¼ cup honey

continued

1. Clean the vegetables and chop them into pieces approximately ½ inch thick. Put them into a large nonreactive bowl (no aluminum, copper, or non-enameled cast iron). Add the salt and toss to combine. Cover and leave 8 hours or overnight, no longer than 24 hours. If it is warmer than 70°F in your home, store the salted vegetables in your refrigerator until moving on to the next step.

2. Rinse the salted vegetables under cold water. Drain and put in a nonreactive pot along with the other ingredients. Bring to a boil, then remove from the heat immediately.

3. Skim off any foam. Use a slotted spoon to pack the piccalilli into clean pint or half-pint canning jars, leaving ½ inch of head space. Pour the still-hot brine over it. You want to completely cover the vegetables in the brine, but still leave at least ½ inch of head space between the surface of the brine and the rim of the jar.

4. Wipe the rim of the jar dry with a clean cloth. Affix canning lids and process in a boiling water bath (page 28) for 10 minutes. Adjust the canning time if you live at a high altitude. Alternatively, skip the canning process and immediately transfer the jars of piccalilli to your refrigerator.

5. Wait at least 1 month for the flavors to mature before enjoying alongside your "Ploughman's Lunch."

Change It Up: The cauliflower and green beans are traditional in piccalilli, but zucchini or other summer squash, sweet peppers, and tomatillos work well, too.

Citrusy Celery Relish

PREPARATION TIME: 10 minutes   WAIT TIME: 4½ hours, including initial salting time

YIELD: Makes 1 pint

With crisp texture and bright flavors, this relish can be served as a side dish as well as a condiment. Serve it on top of fish, add it to potato or egg salads, or sprinkle it over green salads (especially ones that include slightly bitter greens such as arugula or dandelion). It's ready to eat in just a few hours but will keep in your refrigerator for at least a month.

INGREDIENTS

2 cups finely chopped celery stalks

¼ cup minced parsley

¼ cup thinly sliced and chopped citrus (lime, lemon, orange, sour orange, kumquat . . . you decide)

2 tablespoons juice of the same type of citrus you are using

1 teaspoon kosher or other non-iodized salt

½ teaspoon ground cumin

½ cup rice vinegar

½ cup filtered or unchlorinated water

1 tablespoon granulated sugar OR 2 teaspoons agave nectar

½ teaspoon Dijon or other smooth prepared mustard

INSTRUCTIONS

1. Chop the celery no thicker than ⅛ inch. If the stalks are skinny, simply cut crosswise into crescent-shape slivers. If the stalks are hefty, first cut them vertically, then crosswise.

2. In a medium bowl, toss together the celery, parsley, sliced citrus, citrus juice, salt, and cumin. Let sit at room temperature for 30 minutes.

3. In a small pot, combine the vinegar, water, sugar or agave nectar, and mustard. Bring to a boil over medium-high heat, whisking to dissolve the sugar and mustard. As soon as the mixture comes to a boil, remove it from the heat. Let cool for 10 minutes.

4. Pack the celery mixture into a clean glass jar. Pour the slightly cooled but still fairly hot pickling liquid over the celery. Use the back of a spoon to press out any air bubbles. The celery should be fully immersed in the liquid.

5. Store your Citrusy Celery Relish in the refrigerator. Wait at least 4 hours before serving.

Change It Up: Use some of the celery leaves instead of, or in addition to, the parsley. Try chard ribs instead of the celery. Add some cilantro and/or coriander seeds. A scallion or two—green as well as white parts—is good here as well.

Sweet Red Pepper Relish

PREPARATION TIME: 35 minutes   OPTIONAL CANNING TIME: 10 minutes
WAIT TIME: 1 week, including initial salting time   YIELD: Makes 4 half-pint jars

Sweet Pepper Relish is a staple in the cuisines of the southeastern regions of the United States. Colorful and tasty, it is served as part of a cheesy dip as well as on sandwiches.

INGREDIENTS

6 large red bell peppers

2 medium to large onions

2 tablespoons kosher or other non-iodized salt

1½ teaspoons cornstarch

½ cup cider vinegar

½ teaspoon celery seed

½ teaspoon turmeric

⅛ teaspoon freshly ground nutmeg

⅛ teaspoon freshly ground black pepper

¾ cup granulated sugar OR ½ cup light honey (orange blossom, clover, or wildflower honey works well)

INSTRUCTIONS

1. Slice off the stems of the red bell peppers. Cut them in half and remove the seeds and any white pith. Peel the onions and slice off the ends. Finely chop the red peppers and onions or pulse them a few times in a food processor.

2. Combine the peppers and onions in a large bowl. Add the salt and mix well. Don't worry if it seems like a lot of salt—you'll be rinsing most of it off in the next step. The salt will draw water out of the vegetables, which will result in a better taste and texture in the finished relish.

3. Cover the bowl of salted vegetables and leave it in the refrigerator overnight or for 8 to 12 hours.

4. Put the vegetables into a finely meshed sieve and let them drain for a couple of minutes. Rinse them under cold water and then let them drain again for another minute or two. Press on the vegetables with the back of a wood spoon or your clean hands to remove as much liquid as possible.

5.   In a large pot, whisk the cornstarch into the cider vinegar. Add the spices and sugar or honey and bring the mixture to a boil over medium heat, stirring to dissolve the sugar or honey.

6.   Once the spiced vinegar syrup is boiling, add the minced vegetables. Bring the mixture back to a boil, then reduce the heat and simmer, stirring occasionally, for 10 minutes.

7.   Spoon the relish into clean, hot jars. Press down on the relish with the back of a spoon or your clean fingers to release any air bubbles. Either refrigerate immediately or proceed to the next step.

8.   If you plan on canning the relish for long-term storage at room temperature, leave ½ inch of head space between the surface of the food and the rims of the jars. It is not necessary to sterilize the jars for this recipe. Screw on the canning lids and process the relish in a boiling water bath (page 28) for 10 minutes. Adjust the canning time if you live at a high altitude. Once canned in a boiling water bath, the relish will keep inside the sealed jars at room

temperature for at least a year. Once opened, the relish will keep in the refrigerator for up to 3 months.

9.   Wait at least a week for the flavors to combine and mellow before serving the relish.

Change It Up: Use yellow or orange sweet peppers instead of red. The flavor will be almost identical, but the color variations are fun.

Coconut Relish

PREPARATION TIME: 10 to 20 minutes, depending on whether you are starting with an already hulled coconut   WAIT TIME: 24 hours   YIELD: Makes approximately 2 cups

Traditionally served with hot rice and ghee (clarified butter), this unique pickle is also good on fish, as well as on simply steamed sweet potatoes.

You'll need to get your hands on a fresh, ripe coconut for this recipe. If you don't live in a place where coconut palms grow (sigh), you can sometimes find them at large supermarkets and health food store chains.

INGREDIENTS

1 ripe fresh coconut, hulled

3 small, green hot chile peppers OR 1 teaspoon red pepper flakes

1 teaspoon ground coriander seeds

¼ teaspoon ground turmeric

1 tablespoon coconut oil

¼ cup rice wine vinegar

Juice of 1 lime

1 tablespoon granulated sugar OR 2 teaspoons light honey (clover or wildflower honey works well here)

½ teaspoon minced fresh ginger

½ teaspoon kosher or other non-iodized salt

INSTRUCTIONS

1. Usually the fibrous coconut hull has already been removed when you buy a coconut. I'm not talking about the brown shell with a few fibers still attached, but the smooth-surfaced, 1-inch-thick or several-inches-thick hull. If that is still there, whack it off with a large knife (or a machete, if you just happen to have one of those hanging around).

Next, carve out a hole in the hulled coconut and pour out the coconut water (drink this—it is delicious and very healthy).

2. Crack the coconut open with a hammer. With a small knife, carve out the white flesh from the hard shell. It will most likely come off with a brown membrane still attached to one side. No need to remove that layer for this recipe.

3. Chop the coconut into approximately ½-inch dice.

4. If using fresh chile peppers, remove the stems and mince them. Include the seeds for a spicier relish.

5. Heat a skillet over medium heat for a few minutes. Add the ground coriander and the chile peppers or red pepper flakes to the hot, dry pan. Cook, stirring, until fragrant (about 1 minute). Add the turmeric powder and stir for 30 seconds more.

6. Add the oil and the coconut pieces. Cook, stirring constantly, for about 5 minutes until the coconut pieces start to brown but are not burnt. Remove from the heat and let cool completely.

7. Put the rice wine vinegar, lime juice, and sugar or honey in a small bowl. Whisk to dissolve the sugar or honey. Transfer to a food processor and add the coconut and spice mixture along with the minced fresh ginger. Pulse several times to break up the coconut pieces. It should not become a paste but it should be in small enough pieces for the coconut to combine with the liquid.

8. Pack into a sterilized jar (see "How to Sterilize Jars," page 28). Cover and refrigerate. Wait at least 24 hours before serving.

Change It Up: You can make a version of this with dried coconut. It will not be the same, but it will be good (just a sundried tomato is not interchangeable with a fresh tomato but is still good in its own way). Do not fry the dried coconut in the pan with the spices. Instead, rehydrate it in a little hot coconut milk for 20 minutes and mash it together with the fried spices, vinegar, citrus, and sugar or honey.

Tip: Coconut relish only keeps for about a week in the refrigerator. To keep longer, transfer it to freezer containers and freeze for up to 6 months.

KETCHUP

Although tomato ketchup is the only kind most people are aware of, in India, where ketchup originated there are numerous varieties of it. It is usually used as a condiment with meat, but ketchup can also be incorporated in salad dressings, in dips, and as a tasty baked-in spread over meats (yes, like the baked-in ketchup on the top of traditional meatloaf).

Before we get to some ketchups you may never have tried, let's tackle the version that everyone already has high expectations of.

Real Tomato Ketchup

PREPARATION TIME: 1 hour 10 minutes   OPTIONAL CANNING TIME: 10 minutes   WAIT TIME: 2 weeks
YIELD: Makes approximately 1 quart

This ketchup tastes enough like the most famous commercial brand to qualify as "real" ketchup with most people. But the extra step of roasting (okay, technically baking) the tomatoes gives this recipe a "wow" factor the store brand can't match. It is easy to make, and it makes a fun and unexpected gift ("You *made* ketchup?!").

You can skip the roasting step and still end up with good ketchup. But slow-cooking tomatoes in the oven turns even mediocre supermarket tomatoes into great ketchup. It turns ripe, in-season tomatoes into something even more sublime.

INGREDIENTS

2 pounds tomatoes

2 tablespoons extra virgin olive oil

1 cup chopped onion

1 cup chopped celery

¼ cup chopped bell or other sweet pepper

1 tablespoon finely chopped garlic

1 teaspoon tomato paste

⅓ cup filtered or unchlorinated water

2 teaspoons whole coriander seeds OR ¾ teaspoon ground coriander seed

¾ teaspoon chopped fresh ginger

½ teaspoon ground black pepper

⅛ teaspoon ground cloves

1 cup lightly packed fresh basil

¾ cup cider vinegar

¼ cup plus 1 tablespoon brown sugar

½ teaspoon kosher or other non-iodized salt

continued

INSTRUCTIONS

1. If using cherry tomatoes, leave whole. If using larger tomatoes, remove any tough stem ends with the tip of a paring knife. Toss with 1 tablespoon of the olive oil and spread on a baking sheet. Bake at 400°F until the tomatoes collapse and start to brown in spots, about 15 minutes.

2. Heat the remaining tablespoon of olive oil in a heavy-bottomed pot (the ketchup will scorch in a lightweight pot) over medium heat. Add the onion, celery, and sweet pepper. Cook, stirring until the vegetables have softened and the onion is becoming translucent.

3. Add the garlic and tomato paste and cook, stirring constantly, for 1 minute more.

4. Add the water, coriander, ginger, black pepper, and cloves. Simmer for 15 minutes, adding a little more water only if the mixture starts to get dry and stick to the pot.

5. Combine the spice and vegetable mixture together with the tomatoes and basil in a blender or food processor (in a blender, you may need to do this in two batches). Puree until smooth.

6. Rub the mixture through a fine-meshed sieve with the back of a wooden spoon or your clean fingers to remove any tomato seeds or rough particles. I know, I know: this step is a pain in the ass. But if you want the glossy texture of commercial ketchup, this is what you will need to do. And, no, a food mill won't suffice.

7. Put the puree into a pot along with the vinegar, brown sugar, and salt. Simmer, stirring almost constantly, until the mixture is reduced to the thickness of your favorite ketchup. Taste, and add more salt if needed.

8. If you will be immediately refrigerating rather than canning your ketchup, spoon or funnel it into sterilized jars or bottles and refrigerate immediately. For longer storage at room temperature, fill pint or half-pint jars (it is not necessary to sterilize the jars for this version), leaving ½ inch of head space. Process in a boiling water bath (page 28) for 10 minutes. Adjust the canning time if you live at a high altitude.

9. Wait at least 2 weeks for the flavors to mix and mellow before serving.

Tip: You can use the stems from a bunch of fresh basil in this recipe as well as the leaves. Just be sure to finely chop them before measuring.

Change It Up: Use yellow or green tomatoes instead of red ones and leave out the tomato paste.

Mushroom Ketchup

PREPARATION TIME: 2 hours   OPTIONAL CANNING TIME: 10 minutes   WAIT TIME: 1 week, plus 24 hours' initial salting time, including rehydrating time for the porcini   YIELD: Makes approximately 3 cups

Mushroom ketchup was a standby in British kitchens long before tomato ketchup became the most popular kind. Usually thinner than tomato ketchup, mushroom ketchup is a dark brown sauce packed with *umami* flavors. It tastes a bit like Worcestershire sauce, but with its own soy sauce-like twist.

You can serve mushroom ketchup with meat, but I think it is most valuable as an ingredient in vegan soups and other dishes, where it contributes a smoky richness.

INGREDIENTS

2½ pounds fresh mushrooms, sliced

2½ tablespoons kosher or other non-iodized salt

2 ounces dried porcini mushrooms

¾ cup red wine vinegar

¼ cup red wine

⅓ cup finely chopped shallots

2 tablespoons raw demerara sugar

1-inch piece fresh ginger, peeled and sliced into thin coins

1 bay leaf

1 teaspoon whole black peppercorns

1 teaspoon whole allspice

¼ teaspoon freshly ground nutmeg

3 whole cloves

continued

INSTRUCTIONS

1. Toss the fresh mushroom slices with the salt in a large nonreactive bowl (no aluminum, copper, or non-enameled cast iron). Cover, and leave in the refrigerator for 24 hours. Several times during this salting stage, stir the mushrooms and press down on them with the back of a wooden spoon. You are encouraging them to give up their liquid.

2. Bring 1 cup of water to a boil. Pour it over the dried porcini mushrooms and let them soak for at least 30 minutes, or as long as 1 hour.

3. Strain, reserving the soaking liquid. Pour the soaking liquid through a cloth or paper filter to remove any grit.

4. Put the salted mushrooms into a nonreactive pot along with any liquid that the salt drew out of them. Add the rehydrated porcini mushrooms and their filtered soaking liquid, along with the vinegar, red wine, shallots, and sugar.

5. Tie the ginger, bay leaf, peppercorns, allspice, nutmeg, and cloves up into a cheesecloth bundle. Add the spice bundle to the other ingredients in the pot.

6. Bring to a boil over high heat. Reduce the heat and simmer, stirring frequently, for 1 hour and 15 minutes.

7. Remove the spice bag. Puree the mushroom ketchup (in batches if necessary) in a blender or food processor.

8. Clean the pot to remove any stuck-on mushroom bits. Put the pureed ketchup into the pot over medium heat. Cook, stirring, for at least 5 minutes or until the ketchup is as thick as you would like it to be (keeping in mind that mushroom ketchup is traditionally thinner than tomato ketchup). The amount you have to cook it down will depend in part on how much moisture the fresh mushrooms contained.

9. Transfer the mushroom ketchup to sterilized jars or bottles (see "How to Sterilize," page 28). If the lids are metal, put pieces of waxed paper between the jars and their lids. Store in the refrigerator. For long-term storage at room temperature, process in a boiling water bath (page 28) for 10 minutes. Adjust the canning time if you live at a high altitude. Note that with the 10-minute canning time, it is not necessary to sterilize the jars or bottles first.

10. Wait at least 1 week for the flavors to develop before serving (longer is better).

Change It Up: Use spicebush instead of the black pepper and allspice (see "Useful Resources," page 256). Try dried maitake (hen of the woods) or shiitake mushrooms instead of the dried porcini. Add half of a star anise pod to the spice bundle.

Some Like It Hot

There are those who can't stand even a little chile pepper fire in their food. And then there are those, like me, who almost always have some kind of hot sauce on the table. If you are also someone who likes it hot, this chapter is for you. You'll find both vinegar-based and fermentation recipes here. Spicy pickles, whether fermented or preserved with vinegar, get hotter as they age (I hope that turns out to be true of me, too). This means that a 1-month old pickle that includes chile peppers may have a subtle hint of heat, but that same recipe left unopened for six months may knock your socks off. The takeaway is that it while it is always important to include dates on your labels, it is doubly true with pickles that include chile peppers.

A Pint of Pickled Peppers

PREPARATION TIME: 15 minutes   WAIT TIME: 2 days   YIELD: Makes 1 pint

This is one of the simplest and (if you like spicy food as much as I do) most useful pickles. All you need is two ingredients. Because it is made with full-strength vinegar, you may safely skip canning this recipe.

How hot your pickled peppers will be depends on the type of chile pepper you start out with: habaneros, for example, will be fierce, while the more commonly used jalapeños are hot, but not that hot.

Here I've sliced the chile peppers into thin rings because I find those more useful than whole peppers for most recipes. But if you've got some colorful small chilies that you want to keep whole for visual effect, go for it. Just be sure to prick each pepper with the tip of a sharp knife to ensure the vinegar can penetrate it.

Scatter pickled peppers over pizza, add them to pasta, mince them for curries and spicy sauces. Anytime a recipe calls for a chile pepper, you can substitute some of these pickled peppers.

When you've eaten the last pepper in the jar, use the chile-infused vinegar that is left behind as hot sauce.

INGREDIENTS

2 cups thinly sliced, fresh chile pepper rings (from about 1½ pounds whole chile peppers)

1 cup cider vinegar OR white wine vinegar

1 washed cabbage leaf, horseradish leaf, or grape vine leaf (note that your choice of leaves here does have an impact on the flavor)

INSTRUCTIONS

1. Pack the chile pepper slices into a clean glass jar.

2. Bring the vinegar to a boil, then immediately remove it from the heat. Pour over the peppers. They should be fully immersed in the vinegar, but some will float to the top. Place the cabbage or other large leaf (or piece of a leaf) over the peppers. Use a chopstick or the back of a spoon to tuck the edges of the leaf down around the peppers. The leaf is there to keep the peppers immersed in the vinegar.

3. Cover the jar and store in the refrigerator (or a cool cellar will do if you're lucky enough to have one). Will keep indefinitely, although the peppers will soften in texture and lose some color over time.

4. Wait at least 2 days before serving.

Change It Up: As mentioned above, simply changing the kind of chile pepper you are using will drastically change the heat of your pickled peppers (see "Useful Resources" for a link to the heat levels of different chile varieties). You can add some additional flavor layers by tucking any of the following into the jar:

1 garlic clove, lightly smashed

1 sprig cilantro

1 sprig thyme

½ teaspoon whole mustard seeds

½ teaspoon spicebush berries

Tip: Because this is a full-strength vinegar preserve, it is not necessary to process it in a boiling water bath to seal the jars. However, also because it is a full-strength vinegar preserve, it is especially prone to rust metal canning lids. You can put a piece of waxed paper between the rim of the jar and the lid, or you can opt for a jar with a non-metallic lid.

Homemade Hot Sauce, Three Ways

There are some excellent store-brand hot sauces out there. So why bother to make your own from scratch? You get to control exactly how much heat and also create well-rounded flavor with the seasonings and pepper varieties you include. Besides, it's fun.

Easy Vinegar-Based Hot Sauce

PREPARATION TIME: 15 minutes
OPTIONAL CANNING TIME: 10 minutes
WAIT TIME: 5 weeks, including initial soaking week
YIELD: Makes 1 pint

This is a foolproof hot sauce. How hot it is depends on two things: the type of chile pepper you start out with (see "Useful Resources" for a website that will show you clearly where peppers fall on the hottest to mildest graph) and whether or not you leave the seeds in. A lot of the fire is in the seeds, so remove them if you want to tone the heat down a bit.

I like to use raw, unpasteurized vinegar for this recipe and prefer not to can it, so that it retains all the health benefits of a live vinegar. But it works with pasteurized vinegar as well.

The optional xanthan gum thickens the sauce slightly and keeps it from separating.

You can mail order it if it isn't available near you (see "Useful Resources," page 256). The wonderfully spicy flavor will be the same without the xanthan gum, but then you'll need to shake the bottle before using the sauce.

INGREDIENTS

2 cups chopped hot chile peppers

1 cup cider vinegar

¼ cup chopped onion

1 teaspoon chopped garlic

⅛ teaspoon xanthan gum (optional)

INSTRUCTIONS

1. Place the peppers, vinegar, onion, and garlic in a clean glass jar (it is not necessary to sterilize the jar for this recipe). If the peppers float up out of the vinegar, tuck a large piece of a cabbage leaf over the peppers to hold them under the liquid (it helps to use a chopstick to tuck the edges down along the sides of the jar).

2. Cover and let sit for 1 week. Puree the mixture in a blender until smooth.

3. If you are using the optional xanthan gum, first dissolve it in a tablespoon of water. With the blender running, add the xanthan gum mixture to the rest of the hot sauce and let the blender continue to run for at least 1 minute.

4. Transfer to a jar or bottle. If canning, process in a boiling water bath (page 28) for 10 minutes. Adjust the canning time if you live at a high altitude. Otherwise, store your hot sauce in the refrigerator.

5. The hot sauce is technically ready to use as soon as you have finished making it. But it will have a less vinegary, more well-rounded flavor to go with the heat if you wait at least a month before sampling it.

Change It Up: For milder heat, try using up to 50 percent sweet peppers instead of hot chile peppers.

Fermented Hot Sauce

PREPARATION TIME: 10 minutes
WAIT TIME: 3 to 7 days
YIELD: Makes 2 pints

This is another beautifully easy hot sauce to make. It has some tanginess from the fermentation, but without the in-your-nose sharpness of the vinegar in the previous recipe. As with all hot sauces, the heat will be more or less depending on the kind of chile pepper you use, and whether or not you leave in the seeds (remove them for a milder sauce).

INGREDIENTS

1 tablespoon kosher or other non-iodized salt
1 pint filtered or unchlorinated water
3 cups minced chile peppers

INSTRUCTIONS

1. Dissolve the salt in the water (remember that this is a ferment and so it is important to use non-chlorinated water).

2. Put the peppers into a nonreactive jar or crock (no aluminum, copper, or non-enameled cast iron). Pour the brine over the peppers. Press down on the peppers with the back of a spoon to fully immerse them in the brine and to release any air bubbles.

Loosely cover the jar or crock and place it on a plate to catch any overflow during fermentation.

3. Leave the brined peppers to ferment at room temperature for at least 3 days but as long as 1 week. At least once a day, remove the lid and look for signs that the peppers are fermenting. Press down on them lightly with the back of a spoon. You should see some froth or bubbles come up on the surface of the liquid. The ferment will develop the lightly sour smell typical of lacto-fermentation, but because these are chile peppers, the aroma will also have a spicy kick.

4. Once the peppers have been actively fermenting for at least a few days, you can transfer them to the refrigerator as is, keeping the almost relish-like texture. Or you can puree the sauce before refrigerating it. They won't need the plate under them anymore once they are in cold storage. The flavor of the hot sauce will continue to develop over time, and it will keep, chilled, for at least a year. I do not recommend canning a fermented food such as this, because that would destroy its probiotic health benefits.

Change It Up: Use a mix of hot and sweet peppers for a milder sauce. Add finely chopped onion or garlic to ferment along with the peppers.

Tip: Don't be alarmed if you see some white mold form on the surface of the hot sauce while it is in the room temperature ferment stage. For some reason, chile pepper ferments are especially prone to this. It is not dangerous (see "Troubleshooting," page 249), but it can impart an off taste to your hot sauce. Simply skim it off as soon as you notice it.

Tabasco-Style Hot Sauce

PREPARATION TIME: 15 minutes
WAIT TIME: 8 months to 5 years
(yes, you read that correctly)
YIELD: Makes approximately 1 quart

Although there are hundreds of hot sauces on the market these days, Tabasco is still the one you're most likely to see the waitress set down on your table at the diner. There's a good reason for that: its heat is beautifully balanced with flavors both acidic and mellow.

True Tabasco sauce is made from tabasco chile peppers (*Capsicum frutescens var. tabasco*), vinegar, and salt. The familiar brand is produced by McIlhenny Company of Avery Island, Louisiana, and includes salt mined on that same island. It is fermented and aged in oak barrels for years (yes, like wine). Then vinegar is added to both halt the fermentation and round out the flavor. After further aging, you've got the stuff in that ubiquitous hot sauce bottle on the table at the diner.

But can you make it at home? Yes. And no. Your homemade tabasco sauce will never be quite identical to the commercial stuff. But it will have a similarly well-rounded blend of heat and flavor that could not be derived from a quicker process. (Try to taste test your Tabasco-sauce-in-progress every couple of months so that you understand what a difference the secret ingredients of time and patience are making.)

INGREDIENTS

3 pounds tabasco or ripe, red jalapeño peppers

1¾ cups filtered or unchlorinated water

2 tablespoons kosher or other non-iodized salt

3¾ cups white wine vinegar

1 cup oak or hickory chips (note that these will give very different flavors)

¾ teaspoon xanthan gum (optional)

INSTRUCTIONS

1. Remove the stems from the peppers. If you like your hot sauce truly fiery, leave in the seeds. For a milder sauce, cut the peppers in half lengthwise and scrape out the seeds with a small spoon.

2. Coarsely chop the peppers and put them in a blender along with the water and salt. Blend until the mixture is the consistency of a loose paste or thick sauce.

3. Transfer the mixture to two clean glass quart jars and loosely cover them. You will eventually end up with approximately 1 quart of sauce, but at this stage you want at least a couple of inches of head space in the jars, hence the two jars.

4. Leave the loosely covered jars at room temperature. Open the lids at least once a day (more is better). This releases the gases created by fermentation. For the

week or more, the fermentation will be quite vigorous, as lots of gases are released.

5. When the fermentation noticeably slows, add the vinegar, dividing it between the two jars. Divide the wood chips and loosely tie them into 2 cheesecloth bundles. Press the bundles down into the sauce so that they are completely covered. Refasten the lids, tightly this time.

6. Now comes the hard part: leave the jars in a cool but not freezing place (the refrigerator, or an unheated garage or basement) for at least 8 months but as long as 5 years. (I started tasting mine at 6 months, and there is a huge difference as the ferment ages. I've never made it all the way to 5 years, but I am mentioning that potential because it is how the commercial stuff is made.)

7. Take out the wood chip bundles. Put the sauce into a blender.

8. Dissolve the xanthan gum, if using, in 2 tablespoons of water. Start the blender (it is essential to already have the blender running when you add the dissolved xanthan, or you will end up with goopy globs in your sauce). Add the dissolved xanthan and blend for a full minute.

9. Let the sauce sit in the blender, uncovered, for 1 hour before transferring to sterilized bottles or jars; see "How to Sterilize Jars (and When Not to Bother)" on page 28. There is no need to can the sauce. It will keep in the refrigerator or some other cool but not freezing place for at least 1 year.

Kimchi

PREPARATION TIME: 15 minutes

WAIT TIME: 2 weeks, including 2 to 4 days initial fermentation at room temperature   YIELD: Makes 1 pint

Once only associated with Korean cuisine, kimchi is a fiery condiment that is now added to everything from tacos to grain bowls to pizza.

In Korea, kimchi is made in specially designed ceramic kimchi pots, often buried underground. The reason for that is that the weather there is usually warm, and the temperature is cooler underground, allowing for a steadier fermentation. I once knew a guy who buried kimchi pots in his backyard in Brooklyn, NY, to duplicate the process. I didn't have the heart to tell him that his refrigerator would have worked just as well.

Many ingredients find their way into Korean kimchi pots, from hot chile peppers to raw fish (yes, I said raw fish). Recipes vary from family to family.

What is consistent in all kimchi recipes is that they are fermented in much the same way as sauerkraut. And like sauerkraut, kimchi is made mostly out of cabbage. Radishes are a common addition to the cabbage, as well as strong seasonings, including a lot of garlic.

INGREDIENTS

3 cups filtered or unchlorinated water

2 teaspoons kosher or other non-iodized salt

½ teaspoon soy sauce OR *nam pla* (fish sauce)

¾ pound thinly sliced cabbage

¼ pound radishes OR young turnips, cut into slivers

⅓ cup thinly sliced onion

3 garlic cloves, sliced

1 teaspoon grated fresh ginger root

1 to 2 chile peppers OR ½ to 1 teaspoon red pepper flakes

INSTRUCTIONS

1. Combine the filtered or non-chlorinated water with the salt and stir to dissolve. Stir in the soy sauce or the *nam pla*. Remember that it is important the water be non-chlorinated for a successful fermentation to occur (see "Lacto-Fermentation: How It Works," page 21).

2. Put the cabbage, radishes or turnips, onion, garlic, ginger, and chile peppers or red pepper flakes in a large bowl and toss to combine them well. Firmly pack the vegetables and spices into a clean glass pint jar, leaving about ¼ inch of head space.

3. Pour the brine over the food in the jar. Use your clean fingers or the back of a spoon to press down on the food and release any air bubbles. The brine should completely cover the vegetables and spices. If the food starts to float up out of the brine, you can weigh it down with a smaller glass jar filled with water (set the smaller jar directly on top of the food). Or you can simply fill the jar all the way to the rim, leaving no head space at all, and then put a lid loosely on top of the jar. The lid will hold the food under the brine (remember that because you are not canning this recipe, you don't need head space in the jar to enable a vacuum seal). But don't screw the lid on tightly, because you want the gases that develop during fermentation to be able to escape. Another trick is to tuck a cabbage leaf over and around the food to keep it under the brine.

4. Set the jar on a small plate, because it will probably overflow a bit once fermentation kicks in.

5. Leave the kimchi out at room temperature for 2 to 4 days. Every day, take the lid, leaf, or smaller bottle cover off and look for signs of fermentation. You should start to see bubbles on the surface. You'll see these especially if you press gently on the food. But don't just use your eyes: also get close with your nose and sniff for that clean but tangy pickled smell that means the safe, tasty, and healthy fermentation you're after is happening. Because this is kimchi, the aroma will also be pungent with the scent of the garlic and other seasonings.

6. When the kimchi shows the clear signs of fermentation described above, let it remain at room temperature for one more day, then transfer it to the refrigerator or to a cold, dark cellar (or, okay, you could bury it in your backyard). You won't need the plate under the jar any longer because the cold storage temperature will slow down fermentation so much that there shouldn't be any overflow. But you will need to remove the bottle-weight or cabbage leaf cover, if you used one, and replace it with the jar lid.

continued

7. Your kimchi will be ready to sample in 1 to 2 weeks and will keep in cool temperatures for at least one year. The taste will continue to get stronger as your kimchi ages. It's fun to label a few different batches with the date when you started them and then compare tastes as the months go by.

Change It Up: You can add other spices, including black peppercorns, spicebush, peppergrass, and mustard seeds. You can also use root vegetables other than radishes (carrots and burdock are good), and sturdy leaves such as kale instead of the cabbage.

Tip: Kimchi has the power to permanently infuse even glass jars with its pungent aroma. Dedicate a jar (or several) to kimchi and nothing but kimchi.

Costa Rican Spicy Mixed Pickle (*Chilero*), Two Ways

Walk into any "soda" (small family restaurant) in Costa Rica and odds are you'll find a jar of fiery homemade pickles on the table. Same deal at any *pupusa* restaurant in El Salvador.

Each family has their own blend, but what is consistent is a mix of vegetables in a lightly sour liquid made spicy by the inclusion of chile peppers. Called *chilero* or *chilera* in Costa Rica, and *curtido* or *encurtido* in El Salvador, these pickles are addictively good. You control how hot or not they are with the kind and quantity of chile peppers you use.

Chilero is usually made with banana vinegar. But since most of us don't have access to banana vinegar, here I've used live apple cider vinegar for one chilero recipe, and lacto-fermentation to preserve the second chilero recipe. The flavors are just as excellent as in the food I have eaten at the *tico* restaurants in Costa Rica. But if you want to have a go at making your own banana vinegar, I've included instructions below.

Chilero is also sometimes pureed into a hot sauce. If you decide to try this, first make the pickle and let it age for a week (or even better, a month). Then puree the vegetables in a food processor or blender with enough of their brine to make a smooth, pourable sauce.

Serve chilero with *gallo pinto* (rice and beans) or scrambled eggs or . . . honestly, I could eat this with almost any savory dish.

continued

El Vinagre Chilero

PREPARATION TIME: 30 minutes

WAIT TIME: 1 week

YIELD: Makes 1 quart

This is a traditional version of *chilero*. Feel free to use other vegetables than the ones listed here: in Costa Rica, they use whatever they've got that day from the market or garden. The seasonings are traditionally just garlic and chile peppers, but you can experiment with adding bay leaves, fresh dill, or other herbs and spices.

INGREDIENTS

1 cup peeled, sliced carrots

1 cup cauliflower florets

1 chayote, peeled and sliced (use kohlrabi or zucchini if you can't find chayote)

3 to 6 jalapeños, pequins, OR other hot chile peppers

1 cup thickly sliced onions

2 garlic cloves, lightly smashed

1 lime OR lemon, cut crosswise into thin circles

2 tablespoons granulated sugar OR 1½ tablespoons honey

1 tablespoon kosher or other non-iodized salt

1½ cups cider vinegar (or banana vinegar if you can get it; recipe follows)

½ cup filtered or unchlorinated water

INSTRUCTIONS

1. Bring a pot of water to a boil. Blanch the carrots, cauliflower, and chayote or kohlrabi, or zucchini for 1 minute. Drain and immediately put in ice water or under running cold water to stop residual heat from continuing to cook the vegetables.

2. Pierce each of the chile peppers with the tip of a knife (this allows the pickling liquid to penetrate the pepper).

3. Put the blanched vegetables, chile peppers, onion, garlic, and citrus into a clean glass jar. (Okay, okay: the jar on your table at the Costa Rican restaurant was plastic. They almost always are there. But plastic has both health and environmental hazards. Go for glass.)

4. Dissolve the sugar and salt in the vinegar and water. Pour the pickling liquid over the vegetables. The vegetables need to be fully immersed in the liquid. If they are not, add more vinegar.

5. Cover and store in a refrigerator or another cool but not freezing place. Wait at least 1 week (longer is better) for the flavor to develop before serving.

HOW TO MAKE BANANA VINEGAR

Okay, you want to go hardcore and make your own banana vinegar to create the most authentic chilero? Here's how you do it (I've included a "cheat" at the end for those who aren't going to tackle the full process).

PREPARATION TIME: 10 minutes   WAIT TIME: 3 weeks   YIELD: Makes 1 pint

INGREDIENTS

5 ripe bananas, peeled

Patience

INSTRUCTIONS

1. Put the bananas into a clean nonreactive container (no aluminum, copper, or non-enameled cast iron).

2. Mash the bananas with a potato masher or the bottom of a wine bottle or whatever you've got handy that will do the job.

3. Cover the container to keep out fruit flies, and put it in a cool, dark place such as your unheated basement. Now walk away. Seriously, just walk away.

4. Check your banana vinegar once a week. After the first week, you should see the banana pulp floating above the liquid the bananas have released.

5. During the second week, stir the bananas and liquid vigorously at least once per day (more often is better). You should see the mixture frothing up with bubbles on top when you stir—a sign of healthy fermentation. At the end of the second week, strain the banana-vinegar-in-progress and return it to the nonreactive container.

6. Leave the liquid to ferment at room temperature for one more week, stirring vigorously at least once per day. You should notice the fermentation slowing down by the end of this last week (fewer frothy bubbles when you stir it up).

7. Filter the banana vinegar through a cloth or paper coffee filter or several layers of cheesecloth to remove any sediment. Transfer to clean glass bottles or jars and store in the refrigerator or another cold-but-not-freezing place.

The Cheat: Use banana peels and follow the instructions for "Fruit Scrap Vinegar" (page 240). Just be sure to use organically grown bananas, so that you aren't extracting pesticides into your vinegar.

Pura Vida Chilero

PREPARATION TIME: 30 minutes
WAIT TIME: 10 to 11 days, including initial fermentation at room temperature
YIELD: Makes 1 quart

Although classic Costa Rican chilero is made with vinegar as in the previous recipe, this version has all the probiotic health benefits of lacto-fermentation. And the flavor is just as fabulous.

INGREDIENTS

1 cup peeled, sliced carrots

1 cup cauliflower florets

1 chayote, peeled and sliced (use kohlrabi or zucchini if you can't find chayote)

3 to 6 jalapeños, pequins, or other hot chile peppers

1 cup sliced onions

½ cup thickly sliced cucumbers

1 garlic clove, lightly smashed

1 tablespoon kosher or other non-iodized salt

2 teaspoons granulated sugar OR 1½ teaspoons honey

2 cups filtered or unchlorinated water

2 tablespoons starter culture (see page 24)

INSTRUCTIONS

1. Bring a pot of water to a boil. Blanch the carrots, cauliflower, and chayote or kohlrabi, or zucchini for 1 minute. Drain, and immediately put in ice water or under running cold water to stop residual heat from continuing to cook the vegetables.

2. Pierce each of the chile peppers with the tip of a knife (this allows the pickling liquid to penetrate the chile).

3. Put the blanched vegetables, chile peppers, onion, cucumbers, and garlic in a clean glass jar.

4. Dissolve the salt and sugar (or honey) in the water. Stir in the starter culture, and pour the liquid over the other ingredients. The vegetables need to be completely immersed in the brine. If they are not, add more filtered or non-chlorinated water. (It

is not necessary to add more salt since there is enough in the recipe for one quart jar.)

5. Press down with the back of a spoon or your clean fingers to release any air bubbles.

6. If the vegetables float up out of the liquid, put a grape leaf or a piece of a cabbage, kale, or other large, edible leaf on top of them. Tuck the edges down along the inside of the jar. The leaf should form a cap keeping the vegetables beneath the brine.

7. Loosely affix the jar lid and place the jar on top of a small plate (the plate is to catch the overflow that can occur during fermentation). Leave at room temperature for 2 to 4 days. Open the jar daily to check for signs of a successful fermentation: You will see some bubbles froth up on the surface of the liquid (especially immediately after you press down on the vegetables—or the leaf covering them—with the back of a spoon). The pickle will start to develop the characteristic sour-but-clean taste and smell of a healthy lacto-fermented food.

8. Remember that temperature affects fermentation: in a cool environment, you may need to wait an extra day or so for fermentation to kick in, whereas if it's very warm, the ferment may be ready for the next step after just 2 days.

9. Once fermentation has been actively underway for at least a couple of days, transfer the jar of chilero to the refrigerator. There is no need to keep a plate under it at this point. Wait another week for the flavor of the pickle to develop before eating it. The flavor will get increasingly sour and hot-spicy as it ages (remember that refrigeration slows fermentation, but does not halt it).

Change It Up: Chile peppers and onion are constants in chilero, but the other vegetables vary. In addition to the frequently used carrots, cauliflower, and chayote, try sweet peppers, zucchini and other summer squash, radishes, and green and wax beans.

Tip: The step of blanching the vegetables gives you the right texture for authentic chilero but kills off the healthy bacteria needed for fermentation. That is why you need a starter culture for this recipe.

Pickled Jicama with Cayenne and Lime

PREPARATION TIME: 10 minutes   WAIT TIME: 9 days   YIELD: Makes 1½ pints

Jicama is a root vegetable that is usually eaten raw. Its mild flavor and standout crunch make it perfect for pickling. In Central America and Mexico, jicama is often eaten as a snack with a drizzle of lime juice and a sprinkle of cayenne chile powder. This pickled version takes those flavors and turns them into a fermented treat.

INGREDIENTS

2 teaspoons kosher or other non-iodized salt

2 cups filtered or unchlorinated water

4 cups chopped jicama (from 1 very large or 2 medium jicamas)

1 jalapeño pepper (optional)

2 tablespoons fresh lime juice

1 teaspoon whole coriander seeds

½ teaspoon cayenne powder

INSTRUCTIONS

1. Dissolve the salt in the water.

2. To prepare the jicama, first remove the brownish outer layer with a peeler or paring knife, revealing the pale, crisp center. First, cut the jicama into ½-inch slabs, then further slice it up into dice, spears, or matchstick size.

3. Remove the stem from the jalapeño pepper, if using. Cut crosswise into rounds. Include the seeds and white membranes for a spicier pickle, but leave them out for something milder.

4. In a nonreactive mixing bowl (no aluminum, copper, or non-enameled cast iron), toss together the jicama, jalapeño, lime juice, coriander seeds, and cayenne. Pack the mixture into clean jars.

5. Pour the brine over the other ingredients. The jicama should be completely immersed in the brine. If there is not enough liquid to cover them, mix up a little more brine, using 1 teaspoon of non-iodized salt per cup of non-chlorinated water.

6. Press down on the jicama with the back of a spoon or your clean fingers to release any air bubbles.

7. The jicama must be completely immersed in the brine. If the jicama floats up out of the liquid, put a grape leaf or a piece of a cabbage, kale, or other large, edible leaf on top of it. Tuck the edges down along the inside of the jar. The leaf should form a cap, keeping the vegetables beneath the brine.

8. Loosely affix the jar lids and place the jars on top of small plates or a tray (this is to catch the overflow that can occur during fermentation). Leave at room temperature for 2 to 4 days. Open the jar daily to check for signs of a successful fermentation: You will see some bubbles froth up on the surface of the liquid (especially immediately after you press down on the jicama—and the leaf covering it—with the back of a spoon). The pickle will start to develop the characteristic sour-but-clean taste and smell of a healthy lacto-fermented food.

9. Remember that temperature affects fermentation: in a cool environment, you may need to wait an extra day or so for fermentation to kick in, whereas if it's very warm, the ferment may be ready for the next step after just 2 days.

10. Once fermentation has been underway for at least 2 days, transfer the jar of pickled jicama to the refrigerator. There is no need to keep a plate or tray under the jars at this point. Wait another week for the flavor of the pickle to develop before eating it. The flavor will get increasingly sour and spicy as it ages, so eat it young for a lighter taste, or wait a month or more for it to have more punch.

Change It Up: Use dill or fennel seeds instead of the coriander. Use sour orange or lemon instead of the lime.

Tip: You will start out with two pint jars full of jicama but likely end up with only 1½ pints because the jicama will shrink slightly during the fermentation. You can transfer the fermented jicama to smaller jars or one-pint jar plus one half-pint jar before putting them in the refrigerator.

Pickled Fruit

Pickling fruit is becoming popular again after a few decades off our menus. In many parts of the world, from Japan to Scandinavia, from umeboshi plums to pickled gooseberries, pickled fruit has been on the table all along, and with good reason.

In addition to bringing their own sweetness to the pickle, which is usually of the sweet-and-sour type, fruits give pickles a smooth and rich, but not heavy, flavor that no cucumber ever achieves.

Pickled fruits are the perfect companions for rich meats and cheeses. They are also intriguing as part of a relish tray. (Have I mentioned that I am very much in favor of bringing back the relish tray?)

Cinnamon-Spiced Apple Rings

PREPARATION TIME: 20 minutes   OPTIONAL CANNING TIME: 10 minutes
WAIT TIME: 3 weeks   YIELD: Makes approximately 5 pints

In the not-so-distant past, spiced apple rings were served not only during the holidays, but throughout the winter months. They are the perfect accompaniment to roasted meat and poultry, but also excellent alongside vegetarian casseroles, roasted root vegetables, and baked winter squash.

Yes, you can buy these preserved apple rings, or some semblance of them. But the traditional vinegar pickling element is long gone from the packaged variety, which nowadays are merely drowning in corn syrup with "cinnamon flavoring." And the bright red color, that is the hallmark of store-brand versions of this treat? If you really must have it, you'll need to resort to unhealthy food coloring. Instead, I've used a slice of beet. You don't taste the beet in the final product, but it does give the apples a bright pink, if not red, color.

INGREDIENTS

10 cups filtered or unchlorinated water

¾ cup cider vinegar

5 pounds firm apples

3½ cups granulated sugar

1 small beet, peeled and cut into 5 wedges

10 cinnamon sticks

1 tablespoon whole allspice OR spicebush

1 teaspoon whole cloves

INSTRUCTIONS

1. Combine 8 cups of the water with 2 tablespoons of the vinegar in a large bowl or pot.

2. Peel and core the apples. Cut crosswise into ½-inch-thick rings. Drop the apple rings into the acidulated water as they're ready.

3. Combine the sugar, remaining water and vinegar, beet wedges, and spices in a large, nonreactive pot (no aluminum, copper, or non-enameled cast iron) over medium-high heat. Bring to a boil, stirring to dissolve the sugar.

4. Reduce the heat and simmer for 5 minutes.

5. Drain the apple rings and add them to the spiced brine. Simmer for another 5 minutes.

6. Remove from the heat. Use tongs to remove the cinnamon sticks and put one in each of five jars (you'll be discarding five sticks). The jars should be clean, but they do not need to be sterilized.

7. Put one beet wedge in each jar.

8. Use a slotted spoon to transfer the apple rings to the jars, packing them down a bit. Pour the hot brine over the apples. The apples should be fully immersed in the brine, but still have ½ inch of head space between the surface of the liquid and the rims of the jars. Press down on the apples with the back of a spoon to release any air bubbles.

9. Wipe off the rims of the jars with a paper towel or clean cloth. Affix canning lids. Process in a boiling water bath (page 28) for 10 minutes. Adjust the canning time if you live at a high altitude. Wait at least 3 weeks before serving.

Tip: Don't be concerned if at first the apples aren't very red. The color will develop during the weeks they are in the jar before you serve them. The longer you leave the apples in the jars, the brighter their color will get.

Fermented Sour Cherries

PREPARATION TIME: 15 minutes or more (depending on how many cherries you start with)
WAIT TIME: 2 to 4 weeks   YIELD: varies

These are sublime, paired with a soft, gooey cheese such as a camembert. During the brief season when sour cherries are available in summer, nab a few pints and start a batch of these. (You can make them with sweet cherries as well, but the resulting flavor is not nearly as interesting.)

INGREDIENTS

1 part sour cherries
1 part granulated sugar
Cider vinegar (optional—see instructions)

INSTRUCTIONS

1. Wash the cherries and remove the stems. Remove the pits, either with a cherry pitter or with this handy DIY method: Put the cherry on the top of an open (and empty!) beer or wine bottle. Punch down on it with a chopstick. The chopstick will push the pit out into the bottle.

2. Weigh your pitted sour cherries (they will weigh about a third less than they did before they were pitted). Place them in a crock or bowl and stir them together with an equal amount (by weight) of sugar. Cover with a dish towel. Leave at room temperature for 2 to 4 weeks, stirring gently at least once daily (more often is better).

3. The initial fermentation will be vigorous and frothy. Once it starts to slow down, use a slotted spoon to transfer the now-fermented sour cherries to a clean glass jar, reserving the liquid.

4. Now you have a choice. You can simply cover the cherries with the fermentation liquid and refrigerate immediately. They will continue to ferment slowly, and their flavor will change over time (not

necessarily a bad thing). Alternatively, you can measure the liquid and stir in 2 tablespoons of cider vinegar per cup of liquid. Pour enough of the mixture over the fruit to completely immerse it. Fasten the lid and store in your refrigerator or in a cold cellar. The vinegar stops the fermentation and adds a hint of acidity that is tasty.

Change It Up: Foraging enthusiasts can use ripe wild black cherries (Prunus serotina). Don't bother trying to remove the pits from the tiny fruits; just give your guests a small dish to deposit them in. You can also use this recipe with beach plums (Prunus maritima) or other very small plums no bigger than 1 inch in diameter. As with the wild cherries, don't pit the fruits first. Instead, just prick each plum with the tip of a sharp knife before proceeding with the recipe.

Spiced Pickled Plums

PREPARATION TIME: 40 minutes   OPTIONAL CANNING TIME: 10 minutes   WAIT TIME: 2 weeks
YIELD: Makes approximately 2 pints, depending on the size of the plums

Make these from small (1- to 1½-inch) plums that are ripe but not mushy-ripe. Purple, yellow, red—any variety of small plum will do. Serve them as part of an hors d'oeuvres plate, alongside pork or game meats, with duck, or as a nibble to go with a good, fruity ale.

INGREDIENTS

1 pound firm, almost ripe small plums

⅔ cup balsamic vinegar (supermarket brand is fine— you're going to concentrate it)

1 cup filtered or unchlorinated water

½ cup granulated sugar OR ⅓ cup light honey (clover or orange blossom honey works well)

⅓ cup wine vinegar

1 teaspoon kosher or other non-iodized salt

4 cardamom pods

1 cinnamon stick

1-inch piece fresh ginger root, coarsely chopped

1 whole star anise

1 whole clove

INSTRUCTIONS

1. Use the tip of a sharp paring knife to cut 3 lengthwise slits in each plum. Put the plums into two clean, heatproof jars.

2. Put the balsamic vinegar into a small nonreactive saucepan (no aluminum, copper, or non-enameled cast iron) and simmer until it is reduced by half.

3. Combine the water, sugar or honey, reduced balsamic vinegar, wine vinegar, salt, and spices in the nonreactive saucepan. Bring to a boil. Reduce the heat and simmer for 10 minutes. Remove from the heat and let sit for 5 minutes.

4. Pour the still-hot brine over the plums. It's fine if some of the spices go into the jars along with the brine, except for the star anise, which tends to overwhelm the other flavors over time if left in.

The fruit should be completely immersed in the liquid. If you will be canning the plums for long-term storage at room temperature, be sure there is at least ½ inch between the surface of the food and the rims of the jars.

5. Screw on the lids and either refrigerate immediately (they will keep in the refrigerator for several months) or process the jars in a boiling water bath (page 28) for 10 minutes. Adjust the canning time if you live at a high altitude.

6. Either way—refrigerated or canned—wait at least 2 weeks before serving.

Change It Up: Use small apricots or crabapples instead of plums.

Pickled Star Fruit (*Carambola*)

PREPARATION TIME: 25 minutes   OPTIONAL CANNING TIME: 10 minutes
WAIT TIME: 3 weeks, including initial 12-hour soaking time   YIELD: Makes 2 pints

This recipe has an intriguing pickling liquid that includes beer and cardamom. It pairs nicely with the star fruit's mild tanginess. The eye-pleasing shape of the slices is a bonus. (Put a few slices facing out along the sides of the jar for a terrific gift presentation.)

Try to use slightly under-ripe star fruit if you can find them—they will bring their own sourness to the mix. If you're working with riper star fruit with little sourness, try adding an extra 2 tablespoons of vinegar to the pickling liquid.

INGREDIENTS

4 cups sliced star fruit (*carambola*)

¾ cup cider vinegar

½ cup granulated sugar

⅓ cup lager or pilsner beer

1 teaspoon kosher or other non-iodized salt

1-inch piece fresh ginger, cut in half

4 whole black peppercorns

3 cardamom pods, lightly crushed

3 whole allspice

1 whole clove

INSTRUCTIONS

1. Cut the ends off of the star fruit. Cut crosswise into slices approximately ¼ inch thick. Put the sliced star fruit into a nonreactive container (no aluminum, copper, or non-enameled cast iron).

2. Combine the remaining ingredients in a pot and bring to a boil over medium-high heat, stirring to dissolve the sugar and salt. Reduce the heat and simmer for 5 minutes.

3. Pour the hot liquid and spices over the star fruit. Refrigerate for 8 to 12 hours.

4. Use a slotted spoon to transfer the fruit to clean glass jars. Leave 1 inch of head space.

5. Remove the whole clove. (It's fine if the other spices remain in the jars, but the clove tends to overpower other flavors over time.) Put the liquid and spices back into the pot and bring to a boil. Pour the hot pickling liquid over the star fruit. The fruit should be completely submerged in the liquid with at least ½ inch of head space remaining between it and the rims of the jars.

6. Process in a boiling water bath (page 28) for 10 minutes. Adjust the canning time if you live at a high altitude. Alternatively, store in the refrigerator. Either way, wait at least 3 weeks before serving.

Change It Up: Use tangerine sections instead of the star fruit. If you can get spicebush (see "Useful Resources," page 256), use it in place of the black peppercorns and allspice.

Spicy Pickled Pineapple

PREPARATION TIME: 15 minutes   OPTIONAL CANNING TIME: 5 minutes
WAIT TIME: 4 days   YIELD: Makes approximately 1 quart

This pickle is bursting with tropical flavor from the sweet-and-sour pickling liquid, gloriously ripe pineapple, and a contrasting sizzle from the jalapeño peppers. Use banana vinegar if you can find it for even more tropical flavor (or make your own banana vinegar using the method on page 163).

INGREDIENTS

1 large, ripe pineapple

2 cups banana vinegar OR rice vinegar

1 cup filtered or unchlorinated water

Juice of 1 lime

2 tablespoons granulated sugar OR agave nectar

2 teaspoons kosher or other non-iodized salt

1 teaspoon whole coriander seeds

1 to 2 jalapeño peppers, cut crosswise into circles

INSTRUCTIONS

1. Choose a ripe, aromatic pineapple. Slice off the top and bottom ends, as well as the rind. Remove the core. Cut the remainder into rings, half-rings, or chunks.

2. Put the pineapple into a nonreactive pot (no aluminum, copper, or non-enameled cast iron). Add the other ingredients. Bring to a boil over high heat. Reduce the heat and simmer for 5 minutes.

3. Remove the pineapple pickle from the heat. Use a slotted spoon to transfer the pineapple and jalapeño peppers to a clean, heatproof jar. Pour the

hot brine over the pineapple. Push down on the pineapple with the back of a spoon to release any air bubbles. The pineapple should be completely covered by the pickling liquid.

4. Cover and let the pickled pineapple cool to room temperature before transferring to the refrigerator. Wait at least 4 days before serving.

5. For long term storage at room temperature, first sterilize the jar or jars (see "How to Sterilize Jars," page 28). In Step 3, be sure there is at least ½ inch of head space between the surface of the liquid and the rim of the jar. Process in a boiling water bath (page 28) for 5 minutes. Adjust the canning time if you live at a high altitude.

Tip: You can save the core and rind of the pineapple and use them to make a Fruit Scrap Vinegar (page 240).

Whole Poached Pickled Seckle Pears

PREPARATION TIME: 20 minutes   OPTIONAL CANNING TIME: 10 minutes
WAIT TIME: 1 week   YIELD: Makes 2 pints

Seckle pears are small enough that you can serve several of them per person for an adorable presentation. Rice vinegar and ginger are classic pairings for this fruit. Here I've chosen to use agave nectar for a neutral sweet background, but sugar or a very light honey will also work.

If you can't find Seckle pears (usually available for just a few weeks in late summer and early fall), you can use sliced pear halves or wedges. Just be sure to leave the peels on so that they don't turn to mush during the poaching.

INGREDIENTS

1½ pounds whole Seckle pears

2 cups rice vinegar

1 cup filtered or unchlorinated water

⅔ cup agave nectar

1 teaspoon kosher or other non-iodized salt

1-inch piece fresh ginger, cut into ¼-inch-thick rounds

6 whole black peppercorns

2 cinnamon sticks

2 bay leaves

2 whole cloves

INSTRUCTIONS

1. Wash the Seckle pears and drain in a colander. Pierce each pear 4 to 6 times with a skewer or the tip of a paring knife.

2. Combine the vinegar, water, agave, and salt in a nonreactive pot (no aluminum, copper, or non-enameled cast iron). Bring to a boil over

medium-high heat. Add the prepared Seckle pears along with the ginger, peppercorns, cinnamon sticks, bay leaves, and cloves. When the liquid comes back to a boil, reduce the heat and simmer for 8 minutes.

3. Remove the pot from the heat. Use a slotted spoon to transfer the poached pears into two clean pint jars. Pour the hot pickling liquid over the pears. The pears should be completely immersed in the brine, but there should still be at least ½ inch of head space between the surface of the liquid and the rim of the jar.

4. Cover and store in the refrigerator or other cold but not freezing place. For long-term storage at room temperature, process in a boiling water bath (page 28) for 10 minutes. Adjust the canning time if you live at a high altitude.

5. Whether refrigerated or canned, wait at least 1 week for the flavors to develop before serving.

Change It Up: Use small apples or apple quarters instead of the pears. Replace the ginger with pieces of whole vanilla bean.

Pickled Blackberries

PREPARATION TIME: 1 hour 15 minutes, including cool-down time   WAIT TIME: 1 week
YIELD: Makes approximately 2 pints

These pickled berries are like a cross between blackberry jam and a chutney. They are fabulous with game meats or poultry and also excellent with mild goat cheese or ricotta. Pickled blackberries also pair beautifully with fresh fruits, especially citrus, peaches, and cantaloupe or honeydew melon.

If you are gathering the berries rather than purchasing them, be sure they are fully ripe. If you use underripe blackberries, the final pickle will not have much flavor beyond what is in the pickling liquid ingredients.

INGREDIENTS

2 strips organic lemon zest (see instructions)

2 cups red wine vinegar OR champagne vinegar

2 cups filtered or unchlorinated water

1/3 cup granulated sugar

6 whole allspice

4 whole black peppercorns

4 juniper berries

2 bay leaves

1 whole clove

18 ounces ripe blackberries

INSTRUCTIONS

1. Use a vegetable peeler to take two approximately 1½-inch strips of zest (just the yellow part of the peel) off of an organically grown lemon. It is important to use an organically grown lemon any time the zest is the part you will be eating. (You don't want pesticides in your pickled blackberries, do you?)

2. Put the lemon zest into a nonreactive pot (no aluminum, copper, or non-enameled cast iron) together with all the other ingredients except for the blackberries. Bring to a boil over medium-high heat, stirring to dissolve the sugar.

3. Reduce the heat and simmer for 5 minutes. Remove from the heat and let cool completely to room temperature. Don't try to speed up the cool-down by putting the pickling liquid in the refrigerator. During the cool-down time, the spices are infusing the liquid with their flavors, and you don't want to rush that.

4. While you're waiting for the pickling liquid to cool down, sterilize your jars (see "How to Sterilize," page 28).

5. Divide the blackberries between the jars, leaving about 1 inch of head space. You won't be canning this pickle, because that would reduce the berries to mush. The head space is intended to leave enough room to completely cover the berries with the liquid. Pour the cooled pickling liquid over the berries. Press down on the blackberries with the back of a spoon (very gently, to avoid crushing the berries).

6. Screw on the lids and leave the pickled blackberries at room temperature for 24 hours before transferring them to the refrigerator. Wait at least a full week before serving, during which time the blackberries and spices will get to know each other and the vinegar taste will mellow.

Change It Up: This recipe works just as well with raspberries or mulberries.

Tip: Save the liquid after you've eaten all of the blackberries. Use it as you would a shrub, adding a splash to club soda or cocktails. It is also an interesting addition to salad dressings.

Raspberry Shrub

PREPARATION TIME: 10 minutes   WAIT TIME: 9 days, including 2 days initial maceration time
YIELD: Makes 1½ pints

One step away from pickled berries are berry-flavored shrubs. Do shrubs qualify as a pickle? I may be stretching the definition a bit, but there is acidity and food preservation at work, so never mind.

Shrubs are an old-fashioned beverage concentrate made with fruit, vinegar, and sugar. Add a dash to some club soda and you've got one of the most refreshing summer beverages imaginable. Add a little vodka or other alcohol, and, well, shrubs can open up a whole world of cocktail possibilities.

INGREDIENTS

8 ounces fresh or frozen raspberries

1 cup granulated sugar

1 to 1½ cups cider or sherry vinegar

INSTRUCTIONS

1. Mix together the raspberries and sugar. Cover and refrigerate for 24 hours. Stir well and then cover and refrigerate for another 24 hours. By this time, the sugar will have drawn most of the liquid out of the berries.

2. Strain out the liquid (you can reserve the raspberry solids to make raspberry vinegar). Measure the liquid and add an equal amount of cider or sherry vinegar (or better yet, raspberry vinegar, if you happen to have some already made on hand).

3. Put the mixture into a clean glass jar, cover, and put into the refrigerator. Do not use for at least a week, longer if you can convince yourself to wait. Freshly made shrub is, in my opinion, too segregated in taste to be enjoyable. The vinegar and sugar jump out at your taste buds, muting the fruit flavor. But give it time (3 months is not too much), and the flavors will harmonize. Then you will have an ingredient that is truly pleasurable to work with and to serve.

WHAT TO DO WITH RASPBERRY SHRUB

Try simply mixing it with seltzer or other sparking water. If you want to go for a cocktail, adding some raspberry shrub to light rum is good, with or without ice. But don't let your creativity stop there: You can also use shrubs in marinades and salad dressings.

Spiced Pickled Grapes

PREPARATION TIME: 15 minutes   WAIT TIME: 4 hours   YIELD: Makes approximately 1 pint

Richly flavored due to the spices, these sweet-and-sour pickled grapes have a pleasingly crisp "pop" when you bite into them.
Serve them as part of a relish tray, on top of strong aged cheeses, or instead of the usual raisins in carrot salad.

INGREDIENTS

1 pound seedless grapes

1½ cups cider vinegar

½ cup granulated sugar

½ cup brown sugar

1 cup filtered or unchlorinated water

6 fresh ginger slices, about ¼ inch thick

2 star anise

2 small fresh or dried hot chile peppers

2 cinnamon sticks

2 tablespoons whole coriander seeds

6 whole black peppercorns

1 bay leaf

1 whole clove

INSTRUCTIONS

1. Wash the grapes and remove them from the stems. Prick each grape once with a clean needle or pin. This enables the flavor of the spiced pickling liquid to penetrate the grapes better. Try to pierce the spot where the stem was attached. Piercing the grapes elsewhere could result in the skins splitting when you pour the hot pickling liquid over the grapes, and that would ruin that pleasantly crisp texture I mentioned earlier.

2. Put all of the ingredients except for the seedless grapes into a nonreactive pot (no aluminum, copper, or non-enameled cast iron). Bring to a boil over medium-high heat, stirring to dissolve the white and brown sugars.

3. Put the grapes into clean, heatproof jars. Pour the still-hot pickling liquid over them. The grapes need to be completely immersed in the pickling liquid. Cover and let cool to room temperature before transferring to the refrigerator.

4. Wait at least 4 hours before serving. Pickled grapes will keep, refrigerated, for at least 1 month.

Change It Up: You can use a mix of green and red seedless grapes for a more colorful pickle. You can also make this recipe with blueberries instead of grapes.

Tip: The heat of the peppers and the flavors of the spices (especially the star anise) will intensify the longer you keep the pickled grapes before eating them. That's not necessarily a bad thing, but if you want a milder flavor, remove the chile peppers and the star anise no more than a week after you first make the pickles.

Pickled Cheese, Eggs, Fish, and Meat

Aside from pickled herring, many people are unfamiliar with even the idea (never mind the taste) of pickled animal products. But cultures around the world (including the United States until a few decades ago) have long-standing traditions of eating pickled dairy, eggs, fish, poultry, and meat. In the days before it was usual for most families to have an electric refrigerator in the house, pickling was one of the important ways to preserve these animal foods.

I'm not just sending you down a food history tangent here. These recipes will be a revelation to your taste buds. And if you hunt or fish, pickling should definitely be part of your repertoire when you are determining how to preserve the abundance of your catch.

Pickled Cheese

PREPARATION TIME: 10 minutes   WAIT TIME: 1 week, plus 1- to 4-hours initial vinegar soaking time
YIELD: Makes 1 pint

In parts of Eastern Europe and Russia, pickled cheese is a common sight on the table. It is a way of taking fresh, mild cheeses that would otherwise need to be eaten within a few days and preserving them for weeks or even months. A bonus is that the cheese becomes infused with the flavors of the spices.

INGREDIENTS

1 pound feta, queso blanco, ricotta salata, or other fresh cheese that is young enough to be creamy and mild, but dry enough to be sliceable

2 cups white wine vinegar

1 bay leaf

½ lemon or other citrus, cut into thin slivers, peel included (which citrus you choose radically alters the flavor of your finished product, but that is part of the fun)

¼ teaspoon whole coriander seeds

¼ teaspoon whole cumin seeds

6 whole black peppercorns

1 small hot chile pepper OR pinch of red pepper flakes (optional)

1 cup extra virgin olive oil

INSTRUCTIONS

1. Cut the cheese into ½-inch cubes. Place in a nonreactive container (no aluminum, copper, or non-enameled cast iron) and cover with the vinegar. Let sit for 1 to 4 hours.

2. Strain (you can reserve the vinegar for another use such as salad dressing or marinade).

3. Place the cheese cubes into a clean jar, tucking in the bay leaf, citrus, seeds, and pepper as you go.

4. Cover the cheese cubes completely with the oil. Tap the bottom of the jar firmly against the palm of one hand to release any air bubbles. Refrigerate and wait at least 1 week before serving.

5. Remember that the olive oil will congeal in the refrigerator's cold temperature, so you will need to take the jar out of the refrigerator at least 1 hour before serving, so that the oil can re-liquefy.

Tip: When you've eaten all of the cheese, use the flavorful oil that is left behind. It is wonderful when slathered on bruschetta or drizzled over simply steamed vegetables.

Irish-Style Pickled Eggs

PREPARATION TIME: 15 minutes, plus time to boil the eggs   WAIT TIME: 1 week
YIELD: Makes 6 pickled eggs

Stop in for a pint at a pub in Ireland, and there's a good chance you'll see a jar of pickled eggs on the counter. Nowadays they're often colored with unhealthy food coloring, but this traditional method uses a few slices of raw beet instead. Don't worry if you're not a beet-lover: you don't taste the vegetable in the egg, but you do get the naturally vivid color.

INGREDIENTS

6 large hard-boiled eggs

12 ounces cider vinegar

5 ounces filtered or unchlorinated water

½ large raw beet, scrubbed clean and cut into ½-inch-thick slices

1 tablespoon kosher or other non-iodized salt

1 tablespoon granulated sugar

INSTRUCTIONS

1. Peel the eggs and place them in a clean glass jar.

2. Combine the rest of the ingredients in a pot and bring to a boil, stirring to dissolve the salt and sugar.

3. Remove the beet slices from the hot liquid. Tuck them in among the eggs. Pour the vinegar mixture over the eggs. They should be completely submerged in the liquid.

4. Cover and refrigerate. It takes the eggs a while to pick up the pink color from the beets, so wait at least 1 week before serving. At first the whites will be pink and the yolks still yellow-orange. Left in the liquid longer, the yolks will also turn pink.

Change It Up: Add some whole black peppercorns and a sprig or two of fresh tarragon to the jar.

Tip: Hard-boiled eggs made with eggs that are at least a few days old (or as much as 2 weeks old) are easier to peel than hard-boiled, freshly laid eggs.

Pickled Fish

PREPARATION TIME: 40 minutes   WAIT TIME: 3½ days, including both initial brining times and refrigerated drying time   YIELD: Makes 2½ pints

Many kinds of fish other than the familiar herring or salmon are also great pickled. Often served at brunch, pickled fish is worth featuring at other meals as well. Try it on triangles of buttered rye toast for an open-faced sandwich that is a traditional Scandinavian treat. Or chop the pickled fish into smaller pieces and add it to a hot potato and onion hash (don't chop it too small before pickling, though, or the vinegar taste will be too strong).

IMPORTANT: Pickled fish should be stored in the refrigerator rather than canned, and it should be eaten within 6 weeks.

INGREDIENTS

1¾ cups kosher or other non-iodized salt

1 gallon plus 1 pint filtered or unchlorinated water

5 pounds filleted fish

1 quart white wine vinegar

1 cup sliced onion, divided

4 whole cloves

4 bay leaves

1 tablespoon whole mustard seeds

1 tablespoon whole black peppercorns

2 teaspoons dill seeds

1 teaspoon whole allspice

1 teaspoon red pepper flakes (optional)

1 lemon, thinly sliced

INSTRUCTIONS

1. Dissolve ½ cup of the salt in 2 quarts of the water in a nonreactive container (no aluminum, copper, or non-enameled cast iron). Soak the fish into the brine, in the refrigerator, for 1 hour. Drain.

2. Dissolve the remaining 1¼ cups salt in 2 quarts water. Put the fish into this stronger brine (again in a nonreactive container). Refrigerate for 12 hours. Drain.

3. Rinse the fish off in cold water. Cut into chunks or 1-inch-thick strips.

4. In a large nonreactive pot, combine the vinegar, 1 pint of water, ½ cup of the onion, and the spices. Bring the mixture to a boil, then add the fish. Simmer for 10 minutes until the fish is easily pierced with a fork but not overcooked.

5. Use a slotted spoon to remove the fish from the liquid. Put the fish in a single layer on plates or a baking sheet and refrigerate for 30 minutes to an hour.

6. Pack the cooled fish into clean heatproof jars, adding the remaining ½ cup of onion slices and the lemon slices as you go.

7. Strain the vinegar mixture, then return it to the pot and bring it to a boil. Pour the hot liquid over the fish, covering the fish pieces entirely. Press down

on the fish with the back of a spoon to release any air bubbles. Affix the lids and refrigerate. Wait at least 3 days before sampling.

Change It Up: Use lime instead of lemon slices when packing the jars. Add a few sprigs of fresh dill or cilantro—if you are a cilantro lover—to the jars before pouring the liquid over the fish.

Pickled Pork

PREPARATION TIME: 20 minutes   WAIT TIME: 4 days, including initial brine-cooling time
YIELD: Makes approximately 1 quart

Pickled pork is a must in Creole and Cajun cooking. If you want real New Orleans red rice and beans, then there had better be some pickled pork in the pot! But its uses go far beyond that.

Think of pickled pork as a seasoning rather than a main course serving of protein. Tenderized by its long immersion in the brine, pickled pork practically dissolves into whatever dish it is cooked with, adding a rich layer of flavor. It is excellent in liquid-based, simmered, or boiled recipes including soup, sauces, vegetables (cabbage is traditional), and grains, including, but not limited to, rice.

IMPORTANT: Pickled pork is NOT ready to eat as is. It MUST be cooked first.

INGREDIENTS

1 quart cider vinegar

¼ cup whole mustard seeds

⅓ cup chopped onion

1 tablespoon whole black peppercorns

1 tablespoon whole celery seeds

2 whole cloves

4 whole allspice

1 tablespoon hot sauce (preferably your own homemade, page 152)

2 bay leaves

6 garlic cloves, lightly smashed

1 tablespoon kosher or other non-iodized salt

2 pounds fresh pork, cut into 2-inch cubes or into strips 3 inches long and 1 inch thick

INSTRUCTIONS

1. Put all of the ingredients except for the pork into a large nonreactive pot (no aluminum, copper, or non-enameled cast iron).

2. Bring the brine to a boil over high heat. Remove from the heat and let cool completely to room temperature. It's fine to "cheat" by putting the brine into the refrigerator to cool down.

3. Rinse off the pork cubes under cold water and then pat them dry with a clean dish towel or paper towels. Put the pork into a stainless steel or glass container that can be sealed.

4. Pour the cooled brine over the pork. Use enough of the brine to completely cover the meat. Seal the container with its lid and refrigerate immediately.

5. Wait at least 4 days before using your pickled pork. Remember that it is intended to be used as a seasoning meat, not as a main course. Pickled pork will keep, still immersed in its brine and refrigerated, for at least 3 months.

6. Rinse off the pickled pork before adding to cooking greens, rice and/or beans, and other dishes. Remember that the meat needs time to cook and break apart into the dish, so add it near the time that you start cooking your recipe.

Tip: You can chop the pork, after it is pickled, into smaller pieces, so that it "melts" more quickly. This is especially helpful for recipes with cooking times shorter than 20 minutes. But chop the pieces just before cooking. Keep the suggested 2-inch-thick cube during the pickling process, or the vinegar taste will be too strong in your finished product.

Pickled Chicken (*Murg Achar*)

PREPARATION TIME: 40 minutes   WAIT TIME: 24 hours, including 1 hour spice-rub waiting time and 20 minutes cool-down time   YIELD: Makes approximately 2 pints

Pickled chicken may seem like an odd idea, but in the Punjab region of Northern India, it is frequently served as either a main course or a snack. *Achar* (sometimes spelled *Achaari*) simply means "pickle that includes a spiced oil."

Once you've got a jar of this in the fridge, you've got a fabulous meal for a lazy night when you don't have the gumption to do much cooking. Just cook it for a few minutes and serve it over rice, or with bread (flatbread or *naan* if you want to be traditional), or combine it with some chickpeas and stewed tomatoes (yes, you can use the canned versions of both) for an almost instant curried stew.

INGREDIENTS

- 2½ pounds boneless chicken (see Tip below)
- ¼ teaspoon cayenne powder
- ¼ teaspoon ground turmeric
- 3 tablespoons minced garlic
- 3 tablespoons grated fresh ginger
- ¼ to ½ cup peanut oil
- ⅛ teaspoon asafetida powder (optional but recommended)
- 1 cup chopped onion
- 2 bay leaves
- 2 teaspoons whole mustard seeds
- 1 teaspoon ground cardamom
- 1 teaspoon paprika
- 1 teaspoon nigella seeds (optional but recommended)
- 1 teaspoon whole fennel seeds
- 1 teaspoon whole fenugreek seeds
- 2 cups cider vinegar OR malt vinegar

INSTRUCTIONS

1. Use kitchen scissors to cut the chicken up into strips or chunks approximately 1 inch thick.

2. Mash the cayenne powder, turmeric, salt, and 2 tablespoons each of the garlic and ginger pastes. Rub the spice paste into all sides and crevasses of the chicken. Refrigerate for 1 hour.

3. Heat the oil in a large skillet over medium-high heat. Add the chicken pieces and fry for 3 minutes, stirring to turn the pieces over, halfway through the cooking. Remove the chicken pieces with tongs and set them on a plate.

4. Return the skillet and the oil left in it to the stove, this time over medium heat. Add the asafetida, if using it, and stir briefly. Add the onions and cook, stirring often, until they start to caramelize and turn golden. Add all of the remaining ingredients (including the remaining tablespoon each of garlic and ginger) except for the vinegar and cook, stirring constantly, for 2 minutes.

5. Add the vinegar and raise the heat to high. When the onion mixture comes to a boil, add the chicken and cook, stirring frequently, for 4 minutes. Remove from the heat and let the pickled chicken cool at room temperature for 20 minutes.

6. Pack the chicken into clean jars and pour any remaining spiced vinegar mixture over the meat. Press down firmly with the back of a spoon to remove any air bubbles. Secure the lids and refrigerate.

7. Wait approximately 24 hours for the flavors to develop before serving. Pickled chicken will keep, refrigerated, for at least 2 months.

Change It Up: You can use turkey instead of chicken. Looking for a vegetarian option? You can make this recipe with cauliflower with excellent results. Break the cauliflower up into small florets (no thicker than 1½ inches). Add 1 minute of blanching in boiling water before proceeding with the recipe.

Tip: Although the shortcut to this recipe is using boneless chicken breasts, you'll get a much tastier result if you use dark meat, such as chicken legs.

African Pickled Fish Curry

PREPARATION TIME: 1 hour   WAIT TIME: 4 days   YIELD: Makes approximately 2½ pints

This is a traditional South African dish that will keep for many months in the fridge, ready to serve anytime with a chunk of good bread as an instant snack. It is richly spiced without being spicy-hot, and it needs no other seasoning. It is also good on rice or atop a green salad.

INGREDIENTS

¼ to ⅓ cup vegetable oil OR bacon fat

5 pounds fillets of any firm, mild-flavored fish

4 cups thinly sliced onions

1 tablespoon ground cumin

1 tablespoon ground coriander

1 tablespoon minced fresh ginger

1 teaspoon ground black pepper

½ teaspoon ground turmeric

3 to 5 hot chile peppers, minced (optional)

4 cups white wine vinegar

¼ cup granulated sugar

3 tablespoons honey

2 teaspoons kosher or other non-iodized salt

INSTRUCTIONS

1. Heat the oil or bacon fat in a large frying pan over medium-high heat. When the oil is hot, add the fish. Don't crowd the fish: you may need to fry it in several batches. The length of time you fry the fish will depend on the thickness of the fillets. Flip the fillets over when their edges start to turn opaque and there is a light golden brown color showing when you lift one up with a spatula to peek at its underside. You want the fish to be cooked all the way through. Add more oil, if needed, between batches.

2. Transfer the fish to a plate and set aside to cool. Return the frying pan to the heat. Add the onions, stirring frequently, until they turn translucent but are not caramelized. Add more oil if necessary to prevent them from sticking. Transfer the cooked onions to the plate with the fish.

3. Reduce the heat to low. Add the cumin, coriander, ginger, pepper, turmeric, and optional chile peppers to the pan, and cook, stirring, for 1 minute.

4. Add the remaining ingredients and return the heat to medium-high. Bring to a boil. Reduce the heat and simmer for 5 minutes. Remove from the heat and allow the pickling liquid to cool to room temperature. (It's okay to speed up the chilling time by putting the liquid into the refrigerator.)

5. Put a little of the pickling liquid into the bottom of a clean, heatproof jar. Put in a layer of the cooked fish, then a layer of the onions. Add a little more of the pickling liquid. Continue alternating layers until the jar is almost but not quite full. Top off with more pickling liquid.

6. Press down on the ingredients with the back of a spoon to release any air bubbles. Cover and refrigerate. Wait at least 4 days before serving.

Change It Up: Some families make this with apricot or peach jam instead of the honey. Experiment with using different fruit jams or jellies to replace the honey.

Pickled Nuts, Seeds, Grains, and Beans

You probably don't think of these ingredients when you think of pickles. Let's change that. Just the tip of a knife's worth of pickled seeds can transform a simple dish into something unusual and intensely flavorful. Pickled nuts can be a revelation for your taste buds. Pickled legumes are just begging to be mashed into a flavorful dip or used as your new favorite burrito filling. Add some pickled nuts, seeds, grains, and beans to your pantry and your meals—even the quickest snacks—are about to become something extraordinary.

PICKLED NUTS

Pickled nuts take the flavor and texture particular to each nut and marry it with spices and sourness in a delightful way. Serve them simply atop a salad, cheese, stewed fruit, or even meat.

Pickled Pine Nuts

PREPARATION TIME: 20 minutes   OPTIONAL CANNING TIME: 10 minutes   WAIT TIME: 3 days
YIELD: Makes ½ cup

For a fancy-seeming but easy-to-make treat, slice open a fresh or dried fig and stuff some of these pickled pine nuts inside. They are also excellent on top of cheese.

INGREDIENTS

¾ cup cider vinegar

¼ cup filtered or unchlorinated water

½ cup pine nuts

¼ cup light honey

1 teaspoon kosher or other non-iodized salt

1 teaspoon red pepper flakes (optional)

½ teaspoon whole black peppercorns

1 bay leaf

INSTRUCTIONS

1. Put all of the ingredients into a small nonreactive pot (no aluminum, copper, or non-enameled cast iron). Bring to a boil over high heat. Reduce the heat and simmer for 15 minutes.

2. Transfer the pickled pine nuts to a clean heat-proof jar. Cover and refrigerate. For long-term storage at room temperature, process in a boiling water bath (page 28) for 10 minutes. Adjust the canning time if you live at a high altitude.

3. Wait at least 3 days before serving.

Change It Up: Try using sunflower seeds or pumpkin seeds instead of the pine nuts.

Tip: The pine nuts may start to turn slightly translucent while they are cooking in the pickling liquid. This is normal and nothing to worry about. If you take my serving suggestion of stuffing the pickled pine nuts into dried figs or apricots, you may want to poach the dried fruit first to plump them up.

Pickled Walnuts

PREPARATION TIME: 30 to 40 minutes   WAITING TIME: 4 months (worth it)   YIELD: Makes 1 quart

Both the British and the French claim pickling walnuts as their tradition, and early American colonists did as well.

The flavor of pickled walnuts is often compared to Worcestershire sauce, and that does come close. Serve them with meat or mashed potatoes, or use them as the base for an interesting gravy. You can also shave pickled walnuts over salads, deviled eggs, and cheese.

You need access to a walnut tree for this recipe, because it is made with unripe, green walnuts (ready in late spring or early summer in most places). If you've got a neighbor with a walnut tree, chances are they're letting most of them go to waste and would be happy for you to take some of them off their hands.

INGREDIENTS

1 quart green walnuts, still in their hulls

1 cup kosher or other non-iodized salt

2 quarts filtered or unchlorinated water

1 quart cider vinegar

1 cup raw demerara sugar

1-inch piece fresh ginger, peeled and cut into slivers

1 tablespoon finely chopped garlic

1 tablespoon whole black peppercorns

1 tablespoon whole allspice

½ teaspoon ground nutmeg

½ teaspoon red pepper flakes

6 whole cloves

INSTRUCTIONS

1. First of all, wear gloves for each step of this process. Seriously. There is a reason something called "walnut stain" is used to stain wood: the juice of the green hull surrounding the shell of the walnut darkens almost anything it touches. Your fingers will be brown for days, maybe weeks, if you handle green walnuts without wearing gloves.

2. Prick each of the green walnuts with a long needle or metal skewer. There should be no hint of resistance from any shell forming within the husk. The walnuts should be soft all the way through. If they've already started forming shells, you missed your chance, and you will need to wait for next year (perhaps a few weeks earlier).

3. Make a brine with ½ cup of the salt and 1 quart of the water. Soak the walnuts in the brine for 1 week. Stir them around at least once a day. You may notice some signs of active fermentation, such as frothy bubbles, when you stir the walnuts. This is a good thing.

4. Drain the walnuts. Make a fresh batch of brine with the remaining ½ cup of salt and quart of water. Soak the walnuts in the brine for another week, again stirring daily.

5. Drain the walnuts. Rinse them off under cool water. Spread them out in a single layer on a screen or on trays for 3 days. By the end of this time, they should have turned deep black. (Note that this is NOT the same as the black walnuts I recommend in the Change It Up note below.)

6. Put all of the remaining ingredients into a nonreactive pot (no aluminum, copper, or non-enameled cast iron). Bring to a boil over high heat. Add the walnuts and wait until the mixture returns to a boil. Reduce the heat and simmer for 15 minutes.

7. Use a slotted spoon to transfer the walnuts to a clean canning jar(s). It is not necessary to sterilize the jar for this recipe. Pour the pickling liquid over the walnuts. They should be completely submerged in the liquid, but there should still be 1 inch of head space between the surface of the liquid and the rim of the jar. (If you will be immediately refrigerating rather than canning the walnuts, you can disregard the head space in the jar, as long as the walnuts are submerged in the liquid.)

8. Process in a boiling water bath (page 28) for 20 minutes. Adjust the canning time if you live at a high altitude.

9. Now comes the hard part: wait 3½ months before sampling. I know, I know . . . it's a long time. But the taste after that time is radically different, in a good way, from what it is after even 2 months.

Change It Up: You can make this recipe with "regular" green walnuts and it will be okay. But it is an entirely different, sublime flavor when made with green (unripe) black walnuts. If you've got a black walnut tree in your neighborhood and have been letting those hard-to-crack nuts go to waste every year, here's your chance to do something with them.

Pickled Green Almonds

PREPARATION TIME: 20 minutes   OPTIONAL CANNING TIME: 15 minutes
WAIT TIME: 1 week   YIELD: Makes approximately 1½ pints

Over a million acres in the United States are planted with almond trees. California has most of them, with Arizona and Utah next, but over a dozen other states also grow this tree for its familiar edible nuts. If you live near almond trees, you should be able to get your hands on the green almonds needed to make this treat. And even if you don't, you can sometimes find them at gourmet markets in big cities during the few weeks they are in season.

These pickles, which are a much-anticipated seasonal treat in Eastern Europe and the Middle East, are not made with the mature, hulled nut (shelled or unshelled) that we are accustomed to eating. Instead, they are made with the entire immature nut, fuzzy green hull and all. At the perfect stage for pickling, the hard shells have not yet formed or are barely starting to form inside the hulls, and you can easily bite through the entire thing.

INGREDIENTS

3 cups green almonds, nuts formed inside but still lacking hard shells

½ cup filtered or unchlorinated water

½ cup white wine vinegar

2 tablespoons honey

2 teaspoons kosher or other non-iodized salt

2 bay leaves

½ teaspoon whole dill OR fennel seeds

2 to 4 whole black peppercorns

2 small hot chile peppers, fresh or dried (optional)

INSTRUCTIONS

1. If the almonds are very young (smaller than an inch long), you can skip this first step and leave the green hulls on. Pierce each one with the tip of a paring knife. For larger but still-green almonds, slice off just the tips of the pointy ends. Look for the seam that the hulls have along one side, similar to that of apricots or peaches. Run a paring knife along that seam. Split the hull apart along

the slice, revealing the cream-colored, shell-less kernel within.

2. Bring the water, vinegar, honey, and salt to a boil, stirring once or twice to completely dissolve the honey and salt.

3. Load a clean heatproof jar, or two half-pint jars, with the green almonds, tucking in the herbs and spices as you go.

4. Once the vinegar brine has come to a full boil, skim off any foam that may have formed. Pour the hot brine over the green almonds, herbs, and spices in the jar. Make sure the almonds are completely covered by the liquid. If you will be storing your green almonds as a refrigerator pickle, you can fill the jar all the way to the top. If you intend to can the pickled green almonds, be sure to leave at least ½ inch of head space between the surface of the pickling liquid and the rim of the jar(s).

5. For long-term storage at room temperature, secure canning lids and process in a boiling water bath (page 28) for 15 minutes. Adjust the canning time if you live at a high altitude.

6. Whether you refrigerate your pickled green almonds or take the extra step of canning them, be sure to wait at least a week for the flavors to develop and mellow before sampling.

Tip: Try serving pickled green almonds with an anise-scented liquor, such as arak or ouzo.

PICKLED SEEDS AND GRAINS

Pickled seeds are an underutilized food. They are packed with bright flavor, and although they are not as crunchy as unpickled seeds, they still provide a nice texture contrast to creamy cheeses or chewy sourdough bread. (Think of the texture of the seeds in "whole grain" prepared mustards and you'll have a sense of the mouthfeel I'm talking about.) A tiny dollop of them can transform a ho-hum cheese and cracker serving into something special. They are also excellent with fish, cold cuts, and pasta.

You can make single seed pickles. For example, the pickled mustard seed recipe below is an excellent condiment on its own. But you can also combine more than one kind of seed to create unique flavor blends. Just remember that with aromatic seeds, what you smell is what you will get, taste-wise. Try crushing a few seeds with a mortar and pestle and inhaling a whiff before committing a bigger quantity to pickling. If the scent pleases you, the taste likely will, as well.

Poor Man's Caviar
(Pickled Mustard Seeds)

PREPARATION TIME: 45 to 50 minutes   OPTIONAL CANNING TIME: 10 minutes
WAIT TIME: 1 month   YIELD: Makes approximately 1 cup

I don't know who first called these pickled seeds poor man's caviar (it wasn't me). But I'm willing to bet it was because the texture of the round little seeds, after they've soaked in the pickling liquid, is slightly reminiscent of the texture of some caviars. The taste, however, is not at all fishy, but instead like a prepared mustard with some pop and crunch.

Try tossing some into a coleslaw, spreading some over a steak, using poor man's caviar as a topping for grilled vegetables. I keep finding more and more uses for these simple pickled seeds, and I bet you will, too.

INGREDIENTS

1 cup white wine vinegar

1 tablespoon kosher or other non-iodized salt

1 tablespoon granulated sugar

¼ cup whole mustard seeds

INSTRUCTIONS

1. Bring the vinegar, salt, and sugar to a boil in a small pot. Bring a separate small nonreactive pot (no aluminum, copper, or non-enameled cast iron) of water to a boil.

2. Toast the mustard seeds in a dry skillet over medium heat for 1 minute. Transfer them to the boiling water. Reduce the heat and simmer for 2 to 3 minutes. This step reduces the bitterness that some mustard seeds have. Strain the seeds in a fine-mesh sieve.

3. Add the seeds to the liquid and bring the ingredients back to a boil over high heat. Reduce the heat and simmer for 35 to 40 minutes, until the seeds swell slightly and become tender.

4. Remove the pot from the heat and let the seeds and vinegar mixture cool to room temperature. Transfer the seeds and the liquid to a clean non-reactive jar or container (no aluminum, copper, or non-enameled cast iron).

5. Store your pickled seeds in the refrigerator or another cool but not freezing place. For long-term storage at room temperature, process a half-pint canning jar of pickled seeds in a boiling water bath (page 28) for 10 minutes. Adjust the canning time if you live at a high altitude.

6. Wait at least 1 month before sampling.

Change It Up: Try adding leafy, aromatic herbs during the last 5 minutes of simmering. Bay, fennel and dill greens, and tarragon are all good choices. Use whole coriander seeds instead of the mustard seeds.

Tip: Yellow, brown, and black mustard seeds will all yield different flavors as well as colors. Experiment to see which you prefer. Foragers can also use garlic mustard seeds (Alliaria petiolata) with good results.

Anise-Scented Fermented Seeds

PREPARATION TIME: 5 minutes   WAIT TIME: 2 weeks   YIELD: Makes approximately ½ cup

If you are a fan of anise and licorice flavors, this one is for you.

One of my favorite ways to serve this pickled seed mix is with coconut milk curries. It is also good with sweet potatoes, celeriac (celery root), parsnips, and acorn or other winter squash. Try a little with some chopped celery and red onion for a simple but flavor-packed salad.

INGREDIENTS

½ cup filtered or unchlorinated water

¾ teaspoon kosher or other non-iodized salt

1 teaspoon honey or agave nectar

¼ cup minced fennel bulb

1 tablespoon whole anise seeds

1 tablespoon whole fennel seeds

1 tablespoon fresh minced tarragon leaves

1 tablespoon fresh minced chervil leaves (optional but excellent if you have chervil)

1 star anise pod

INSTRUCTIONS

1. Put the water, salt, and honey together in a small pot. Bring to a boil, stirring to dissolve the honey and salt. Remove from the heat and let the brine cool to room temperature (fine to speed up the process by putting it in the refrigerator).

2. Put the fennel, seeds, and herbs into a small clean glass jar. Pour the cooled brine over the other ingredients. Stir with a small spoon or chopstick.

3. Loosely affix the jar lid and place the jar on top of a small plate (to catch the overflow that can occur during fermentation). Leave at room temperature for 1 to 2 weeks. Open the jar at least once a day (more often is better) to stir the mixture with a chopstick or small spoon, and to check for signs of a successful fermentation: You will see some bubbles froth up on the surface of the ferment (especially immediately after you stir the seeds). The pickled seeds will start to develop the characteristic sour-but-clean taste and smell of a healthy lacto-fermented food. They will also have a strong anise-y scent, in the case of this recipe.

4. Once fermentation has been underway for at least a week, transfer the jar of fermented seeds and fennel to the refrigerator. There is no need to keep a plate under it at this point. Wait another week for the flavor to develop before serving. The flavor will get increasingly sour as it ages (remember that refrigeration slows fermentation, but does not halt it), but interestingly, the anise-y taste becomes more mellow with time.

Tip: You can add other minced fresh herbs and seeds to this ferment. Try sweet cicely, angelica, lovage, or bishop's elder.

MORE SEEDS TO PICKLE

There are many seeds besides those in the recipes here that are excellent pickled. Try dill, nigella, peppercorns, poppy seeds, caraway, cardamom, or fenugreek.

Pickled Curry Mix

PREPARATION TIME: 40 minutes   WAIT TIME: 3 days   YIELD: Makes approximately 1 cup

Curry powders and pastes are blends of many different aromatic seeds and spices. This pickled mix has all the flavor and color of curry powders, but with more flavor pop because of the acidity of the vinegar and the way the flavor of each of the individual seed types stands out. Use your pickled curry mix with any recipe that includes a curry sauce, but be sure to add it sparingly as a topping just before serving rather than cooking it (cooked, it will tend to overwhelm the other ingredients in your recipe).

INGREDIENTS

3 tablespoons whole cumin seeds

1 tablespoon whole coriander seeds

2 teaspoons whole mustard seeds

½ teaspoon whole fenugreek seeds

1 cup cider vinegar

1 tablespoon kosher or other non-iodized salt

2 teaspoons granulated sugar

2 teaspoons grated fresh ginger

1 teaspoon minced garlic

1 teaspoon grated fresh turmeric root OR ½ teaspoon turmeric powder

INSTRUCTIONS

1. Toast the cumin, coriander, mustard, and fenugreek seeds in a dry skillet until fragrant, about 1 minute.

2. Bring the vinegar, salt, and sugar to a boil in a small pot.

3. Add the toasted seeds to the pickling liquid and bring the ingredients back to a boil over high heat. Reduce the heat and simmer for 20 minutes, until the seeds start to swell. Add the ginger and turmeric and simmer for 15 minutes more.

4. Remove the pot from the heat and let the mixture cool to room temperature. Transfer the pickled curry blend to a clean nonreactive jar or container (no aluminum, copper, or non-enameled cast iron).

5. Store your pickled curry blend in the refrigerator or another cool but not freezing place. For long term storage at room temperature, process a half-pint canning jar of pickled seeds in a boiling water bath (page 28) for 10 minutes. Adjust the canning time if you live at a high altitude.

6. Wait at least 3 days before using.

Pickled Wheat Berries

PREPARATION TIME: 1 hour 15 minutes   OPTIONAL CANNING TIME: 15 minutes   WAIT TIME: 3 days
YIELD: Makes 1 pint

Wheat "berries" are simply the whole grain, or seed, of the wheat plant. Yes, they are ground into our most common flour, but they are also a delicious food in their whole state.

Scatter your pickled wheat berries on salads. Add them to bean soups or tacos. Mound a little heap of them on top of a mild goat cheese on a cracker. In other words, anywhere an interestingly chewy, slightly nutty but brightly sour ingredient would be welcome.

INGREDIENTS

⅔ cup wheat "berries"

3 cups cider vinegar

¼ cup honey

2 teaspoons kosher or other non-iodized salt

1 bay leaf

¼ teaspoon ground black pepper (optional)

¼ teaspoon ground cumin (optional)

INSTRUCTIONS

1. Bring a pot of water to a boil. Add the wheat berries. When the water returns to a boil, reduce the heat and simmer until the wheat berries are cooked. (They should be tender but still slightly chewy—this could take as long as an hour depending on how recently harvest the grain is. Older wheat will take longer.) Drain in a sieve, then run under cold water to stop any cooking from residual heat.

2. Spread the cooked wheat on a clean dish towel. Roll up the dish towel and squeeze hard to remove as much liquid as possible. Transfer the wheat to a bowl.

3. Return the pot you cooked the wheat berries in to the stove. Put the vinegar, honey, and spices in the pot and bring them to a boil over medium-high heat. Add the wheat berries and return to a boil. Reduce the heat and simmer for 5 minutes.

4. Strain the wheat berries through a fine-meshed sieve over a bowl (you will want to reserve the pickling liquid). Transfer the wheat to a clean heat-proof jar. Pour the still-hot pickling liquid over the wheat. Press down on the pickled wheat with the back of a spoon to release any air bubbles. Secure the lid.

5. Refrigerate immediately. Or, for long-term storage at room temperature, be sure to leave at least ½ inch of head space between the surface of the pickle juice and the rim of the jar. Affix the canning lid and process in a boiling water bath (page 28) for 15 minutes. Adjust the canning time if you live at a high altitude.

6. Whether you opted for a refrigerator pickle or canning, wait at least 3 days before serving.

Change It Up: Rye berries are wonderful in this recipe.

Tip: Stick to grains like rye and wheat that retain some chewiness even after they are cooked for pickling. Grains like barley and rice that are soft when cooked don't work as well.

PICKLED LEGUMES (BEANS)

Pickled legumes, including lentils, chickpeas, and the varieties we more commonly call simply "beans," are a wonderfully useful addition to your kitchen. They brighten any cooked green or salad, are excellent in sandwiches and burritos, and can be pureed in a blender or food processor for an almost instant party dip or snack.

Pickled Lentils with Dill

PREPARATION TIME: 40 minutes   OPTIONAL CANNING TIME: 15 minutes
WAIT TIME: 24 hours, including cool-down time for the pickling liquid   YIELD: Makes 2 pints

My favorite way to serve these zesty lentils is spooned over cooked greens. They are especially good with slightly bitter greens, such as mustard leaves, dandelion, or broccoli rabe, but they are also good on salads, in wraps and sandwiches, and sprinkled on soup. (Try pickled lentils on lentil soup for a fun variation.)

INGREDIENTS

1 cup lentils (see Tip below)

3 garlic cloves

2 bay leaves

½ teaspoon kosher or other non-iodized salt

3 tablespoons minced red onion OR shallots

4 sprigs fresh dill leaves

1 cup white wine vinegar

⅓ cup granulated sugar OR ¼ cup light honey OR ¼ cup agave nectar

½ cup filtered or unchlorinated water

3 strips lemon zest

1 teaspoon whole coriander seeds

1 teaspoon whole mustard seeds

¼ teaspoon red pepper flakes OR 1 small hot chile pepper (optional)

¼ teaspoon ground turmeric OR ¾ teaspoon grated fresh turmeric

INSTRUCTIONS

1. Check the lentils for any small stones (it's rare to find any nowadays, but it does happen once in a while). Rinse the lentils in a sieve under cold water.

2. Peel and lightly smash two of the cloves of garlic. Put them, along with 1 of the bay leaves and the lentils, into a pot along with 4 cups of water and the salt. Bring to a boil over high heat, then reduce the heat and simmer until the lentils are tender but not falling apart.

3. Drain the lentils. In a mixing bowl, combine them with the red onion or shallots. Transfer the lentil mixture to two clean, heatproof pint jars. Tuck two sprigs of dill into each jar as you load in the lentils. Allow the lentils to cool in the jars, while you make the pickling liquid.

4. Combine the remaining ingredients in a small nonreactive pot (no aluminum, copper, or non-enameled cast iron). Bring to a boil over high heat, stirring to dissolve the sugar, honey, or agave nectar. Remove from the heat, cover, and let cool to room temperature. Do not rush the cool-down by putting the mixture in the refrigerator; it needs the full time at room temperature for the flavors of the spices to infuse the vinegar and water. The reason you cover the pot during the cool-down is to prevent the aromatic oils in the spices from evaporating out of your pickling liquid.

5. If you will be treating your pickled lentils as a refrigerator pickle, simply pour the cooled pickling liquid over the lentils in the jars. Press down on the lentils with the back of a spoon to release any air bubbles and to ensure that the lentils are entirely covered by the liquid. Put the lids on and refrigerate.

6. For long-term storage at room temperature, bring the pickling liquid back to a boil before pouring it over the lentils. Press down on the lentils with the back of a spoon to release any air bubbles and to ensure that the lentils are entirely covered by the liquid. There should be at least ½ inch of head space between the surface of the liquid and the rims of the jars. Screw on the canning lids and process in a boiling water bath (page 28) for 15 minutes. Adjust the canning time if you live at a high altitude.

7. Whether you opted for refrigeration or canning, wait approximately 24 hours before serving.

Change It Up: Use sprigs of fresh cilantro (coriander) or celery leaves instead of the dill.

Tip: Although you can use "regular" brown lentils in this recipe, you'll get a better texture with the tiny green "French" lentils.

Spicy Fermented Chickpeas (Garbanzo Beans)

PREPARATION TIME: 10 minutes, plus 1 to 3 hours cooking time (if cooking the chickpeas from scratch)
WAIT TIME: 10 days, including 5 to 7 days' initial fermentation at room temperature   YIELD: Makes 1 quart

Puree this with a little tahini for a tangy variation of hummus. Or leave the chickpeas whole and enjoy them as part of a pita bread sandwich or a salad topping.

INGREDIENTS

2 pints cooked chickpeas (canned are okay; cooked from dried will taste even better)

½ cup chopped scallions, white parts and some of the green

1 to 2 jalapeño peppers, cut crosswise into ¼-inch-thick rings

1 teaspoon minced garlic

1 teaspoon whole cumin seeds

½ teaspoon ground black pepper

2 teaspoons kosher or other non-iodized salt

1 pint filtered or unchlorinated water

2 tablespoons starter culture (page 24)

INSTRUCTIONS

1. If starting with canned chickpeas, rinse them well in a colander before proceeding to step 3.

2. If starting with dried chickpeas and cooking them from scratch, first soak them in water overnight. Drain, then put into a pot with plenty of water to cover and cook until the chickpeas are tender. This can take as long as a couple hours (less if they were recently harvested).

3. Use a potato masher or the bottom of a wine bottle to very slightly crush the chickpeas. You aren't trying to mash them, just split most of them open a tiny bit so that the fermentation culture has easier access to the starches within the legumes.

4. In a mixing bowl, gently stir the chickpeas together with the scallions, jalapeño peppers, garlic, and spices. Loosely pack the mixture into clean glass jars.

5. Dissolve the salt in the water. Stir in the starter culture. Pour the brine over the chickpeas.

6. Press down on the chickpeas with the back of a spoon to release any air bubbles. The chickpeas must be completely immersed in the brine. If they float up out of it, place a piece of cabbage leaf (or other large edible leaf) over the top and tuck it in around the edges. The leaf should hold the other ingredients under the brine.

7. Loosely affix a lid and place the jar on a plate or small tray. This is to catch the overflow that almost always happens during the early days of an active fermentation. Leave at room temperature for 5 to 7 days. Open the jar daily and check for signs of fermentation—some frothy bubbles should appear when you push down on the chickpeas (or the leaf covering them) with the back of a spoon. The food will develop the pleasantly sour, clean smell of a successful fermentation.

8. When the fermentation slows down after 5 to 7 days, transfer the chickpeas to the refrigerator or another cold but not freezing place. Wait at least 3 days before sampling.

Change It Up: You can use this recipe with other legumes such as white, kidney, or pinto beans. The catch is that these other legumes end up with a softer texture once cooked and then fermented. They are still great in sandwiches or pureed into spreads.

Tip: Because the chickpeas are cooked, and the healthy-for-us bacteria needed for fermentation have been killed off by heat, this recipe relies on the raw vegetables and the starter culture for fermentation to occur. Do not leave these out, but do feel free to swap out the aromatics I've listed for other raw veggies or herbs.

Pickled Boiled Peanuts

PREPARATION TIME: 1½ hours   OPTIONAL CANNING TIME: 15 minutes   WAIT TIME: 1 week plus 8½ hours soak time and 4 to 8 hours cooking time   YIELD: Makes approximately 3 pints

Looking for something unusual to perk up your next stir-fry or Pad Thai? This is your recipe. Boiled peanuts are a traditional, salty, addictively good appetizer in several parts of Asia. They are also added to cooked recipes for texture and taste contrast. They are also popular in some of the Southeastern states in the United States where peanuts are grown.

Tangy as well as salty, and as spicy as you care to make them, pickled boiled peanuts get gobbled up swiftly, which is almost a shame, because I won't kid you, the preparation time to get to traditional boiled peanuts is long, even though the pickling that comes afterward is relatively swift. However, most of that is inactive time during which you can be busy with other projects. To help with that, if you have a slow cooker, now is the time to pull it out.

You can sometimes find boiled peanuts in the freezer or international sections of large supermarkets. The flavor of pickled boiled peanuts made from scratch is noticeably better, but you'll still get good results if you take a little help from the store. If starting with already boiled peanuts, start the recipe at step 5.

One last bit of information, just in case you think I accidentally put this recipe into the wrong section: Peanuts are not actually nuts. They are the underground seedpods of a legume plant, *Arachis hypogaea*.

INGREDIENTS

1 cup kosher or other non-iodized salt

2 pounds raw, in-the-shell peanuts

1¾ cups rice vinegar

2 tablespoons soy sauce

6 garlic cloves, lightly smashed

1 teaspoon Sichuan peppercorns OR whole black peppercorns

6 to 8 small dried hot chile peppers OR 1 teaspoon red pepper flakes (optional)

INSTRUCTIONS

1. Dissolve ¼ cup of the salt in 2 gallons of water. Rinse the peanuts (still in their shell) under running water to remove any dust or dirt. Add the peanuts to the brine. Soak 8 hours or overnight.

2. Drain the peanuts. Put them into a large pot or slow cooker. Dissolve ¼ cup of the remaining salt in 2 gallons of water. Pour the brine over the peanuts. Bring to a boil, reduce heat, and simmer for 4 hours. If your slow cooker doesn't hold 2 gallons of water plus the peanuts, don't sweat it. Mix the brine as instructed and pour as much of it over the peanuts as the slow cooker will hold. As needed, top up with more of the remaining brine, being sure to first heat the brine to a boil before adding it to the cooker.

3. Shell one of the peanuts after 4 hours to test it for texture and saltiness. If it is not as salty as you would want it for a ready-to-eat bar snack, stir in another ¼ cup of the salt. The texture can be anything from as soft as a fully cooked bean (South Carolina style) to still slightly crunchy (Indonesian style). Test again after a fifth hour of cooking. If needed, add the rest of the salt. Keep testing every hour. It can take as long as 8 hours to reach the desired salty softness. This depends in part on how old the peanuts are—recently harvested peanuts require less cooking time than those that have sat in a package on a shelf for months.

4. If you want to stop at the traditional boiled peanut stage, store the peanuts still in their shells in the refrigerator or freezer. To proceed to the pickling part, shell the boiled peanuts.

5. Combine the vinegar, soy sauce, garlic, peppercorns, and chile peppers in a nonreactive pot (no aluminum, copper, or non-enameled cast iron). Bring to a boil.

6. While you are waiting for the pickling liquid to boil, pack the boiled peanuts into clean heatproof pint or half-pint jars. Pour the hot pickling liquid and spices over the peanuts. The peanuts need to be completely immersed in the liquid. If you will be canning the pickled boiled peanuts, be sure to leave at least ½ inch of head space between the surface of the liquid and the rims of the jars.

continued

7. Secure the lids and refrigerate. Or, for long-term storage at room temperature, be sure to use canning jars and lids. Process in a boiling water bath (page 28) for 15 minutes. Adjust the canning time if you live at a high altitude.

8. Whether you opted for refrigeration or canning, wait at least 1 week before serving.

Change It Up: Swap raw cashews for the peanuts. Yum.

Tip: If you include the dried chiliepeppers in the jars, the spiciness of the pickled boiled peanuts will increase over time. If you like it hot, that could be a good thing. If you want a touch of spiciness but not a lot, remove the chile peppers from the hot pickling liquid before pouring it over the peanuts. Or—for somewhere in the middle spiciness— just leave one chile pepper in each jar.

Pickled Herbs

Usually, herbs are among the background flavors that we add to pickling liquid to flavor the main event. But they are worth pickling on their own.

Pickling herbs is a great way to preserve the gorgeous aromas and unique tastes of certain fresh herbs that do not dry well. For example, as much as I love rosemary, the dried version can be like chewing on tasteless pine needles. And dried basil? Not worth the jar it's stored in. But homemade rosemary vinegar is fantastic in a marinade for lamb, and that basil pesto you turned into a probiotic ferment is just as mouthwateringly good on pasta or fresh tomatoes as fresh basil leaves (albeit with its own, different taste).

Pickling herbs is also a great way to avoid food waste. For example, you bought a whole bunch of fresh cilantro for a recipe that only needed a few sprigs. No need to throw the rest out! Turn it into cilantro vinegar or cilantro pesto. I'm sure you can think of many other examples of herbs that are sold in large bunches when only a little is needed for any one recipe.

10 HERBS TO PICKLE

Technically you can use any aromatic herb in the recipes that follow. But these are especially good candidates because they are herbs that lose most of their fragrance and flavor when dried.

Basil	Fennel leaves
Chervil	Parsley
Chives	Rosemary
Cilantro (coriander)	Shiso
Dill	Tarragon

Universal Herbal Vinegar Recipe, Two Ways

Makes 1 pint

Once you have some herbal vinegar in your pantry, you have a delicious short cut to homemade salad dressings and marinades. You also have a way to add flavor layers that can be subtler than those of the herbs on their own (for example, a splash of tarragon vinegar in your three-bean salad is intriguing but not as overpowering as chopped fresh tarragon can be).

If you want to give some of your herbal vinegars away as gifts, I recommend that you include a card with a few uses or recipe suggestions. Too often these gifts gather dust, not because they aren't delicious, but because the recipient isn't sure what to do with them.

Fresh Herb Cold Infusion Vinegar

PREPARATION TIME: 5 minutes

WAIT TIME: 2 weeks

This is by far my favorite way to make herbal vinegar. Aromatic fresh herbs impart a more rounded flavor to the vinegar than dried ones. The method itself couldn't be easier: the only challenge is being patient while the herbs infuse.

INGREDIENTS

1 cup lightly packed fresh, aromatic herb sprigs

1 pint white wine vinegar

INSTRUCTIONS

1. Put the herbs and vinegar into a clean glass jar. Cover and leave to infuse for 2 weeks. If the jar's lid is metal, put a piece of waxed paper between it and the vinegar.

2. Strain out the herbs and bottle the herbal vinegar. Again, be sure that there isn't any metal touching the vinegar.

3. There is no need to test the acetic acid content (page 26) of your herbal vinegar unless you plan

BEST HERBS FOR HERBAL VINEGAR

Although you can use any herb or spice to make an herbal vinegar, tarragon, basil, sage, chives, chervil, beebalm, and rosemary are especially good.

to use it in other pickling recipes. Otherwise, for salad dressings, marinades, etc., simply let your taste buds guide you when you use herbal vinegars.

Change It Up: You can use other vinegars including red wine vinegar and cider vinegar.

Tip: The fresh herbs that you use to make your cold infusion vinegar will lose their green color and start to look like flabby aquarium seaweed after they've infused. Not appealing, right? If you want to add a few sprigs of herbs to decorate the vinegar for gift-giving, first strain out the spent fresh herbs, then add a sprig of the same herbs, but dried. For example, if I made a sage vinegar with fresh sage, I would strain out those leaves and compost them. Then I would add a sprig or two of dried sage, which will keep its shape and color in the vinegar.

Dried Herb Hot Infusion Vinegar

PREPARATION TIME: 5 minutes

WAIT TIME: 24 hours

YIELD: Makes 1 pint

Dried herbs need a little coaxing to give their full flavor to the vinegar. Heating the vinegar does the job. A plus is that with this method, the herbal vinegar is ready to strain and use within 24 hours.

INGREDIENTS

1 pint wine or cider vinegar

¼ cup dried herbs or spices

INSTRUCTIONS

1. Heat the vinegar in a small nonreactive pot (no aluminum, copper, or non-enameled cast iron). While it is heating, put the herbs into a clean heat-proof jar.

2. As soon as the vinegar reaches a boil, pour it over the herbs in the jar. If the jar's lid is metal, put a piece of waxed paper between it and the vinegar. Cover and let sit for 24 hours before straining and bottling.

Tip: The same essential oils that give herbs and spices their aroma are also what gives them their flavor. The takeaway here is that herbs that are not fragrant will not be flavorful, which can happen with dried herbs that have sat in a jar on a shelf for too long. Crush some and take a whiff before deciding if a dried herb is worth using to make an herbal vinegar.

Mint Sauce for Lamb, Pork, Duck, or Roasted Veggies

PREPARATION TIME: 5 minutes with a blender, 10 without   WAIT TIME: 3 days   YIELD: Makes 1 pint

This is an old-time recipe for a liquid sauce that is a perfect complement to rich fatty meats, such as lamb, pork, or duck. Vegetarians can enjoy mint sauce on naturally sweet roasted vegetables such as butternut squash, carrots, and parsnips. It is also excellent on grilled onions.

INGREDIENTS

1 large bunch fresh mint

1½ cups cider vinegar (use raw vinegar for the health benefits if you can)

½ cup granulated sugar

INSTRUCTIONS

1. Wash the mint and strip the leaves off of the stems.

2. Put the mint leaves into a blender or food processor. If you don't have either of those, mince the mint very, very finely.

3. If using a blender or food processor, add the cider vinegar and sugar and process until the mint leaves are very finely chopped up and the sugar is dissolved. If using mint that you minced with a knife by hand, stir the mint together with the other ingredients until the sugar is completely dissolved.

4. Wait at least 3 days for the mint to fully infuse the sauce before serving. Shake well before using.

Change It Up: Use a combination of fresh sage and parsley instead of the mint. (Fresh sage on its own is a bit too strong, but the parsley buffers it nicely.)

Tip: The mint will lose its bright green color in the sauce over time even if stored in the refrigerator. To prevent this, you can briefly (no more than 30 seconds) blanch the mint in simmering water and then immediately chill it in ice water. You will not sacrifice much of the flavor, and the herb will keep its brilliant green hue in the sauce.

Pickled Pesto Ferment

What can you do with this fermented pesto?
Anything you can do with other kinds of pesto. Serve it on pasta, lovely peak season tomatoes, focaccia, etc. Just be sure to add it to the pasta at the last minute, and don't cook it; this will allow you to keep its probiotic health benefits.

INGREDIENTS
1 large bunch fresh basil (about 12 ounces)

1½ teaspoons kosher or other non-iodized salt

½ cup walnuts or pine nuts

3 garlic cloves

1 cup filtered or unchlorinated water

Freshly ground black pepper to taste

1 cup extra virgin olive oil

½ cup grated parmesan or romano cheese (optional)

INSTRUCTIONS

1. Pinch the basil leaves off the stems. (Save the stems for another use, such as making herbal vinegar, page 230.)

2. Put the basil leaves together with ½ teaspoon of the salt, the nuts, and the garlic into a blender or food processor.

3. Separately, dissolve the remaining teaspoon of salt in the water.

4. Puree, adding the liquid brine as necessary to form a not-completely smooth paste. (I like a few chunks of nut still in there for texture.) Mix in freshly ground black pepper to taste.

5. Transfer the pesto to a clean glass jar, pressing down with the back of a spoon to remove any air bubbles. Top the jar with a little of the remaining brine.

6. Loosely cover and leave at room temperature for 3 to 5 days. Check daily for signs of active fermentation (a clean, lightly sour smell; bubbles frothing up to the surface). Stir at least twice daily (this helps to prevent mold).

7. Fasten the lid more securely and transfer the pesto to the refrigerator. Just before serving, mix in the olive oil and optional grated cheese.

Change It Up: Use cilantro instead of basil. Add a dash of hot sauce.

Tip: The basil may darken during storage. This in no way affects the flavor. Unlike the tip for Mint Sauce above, I do not recommend blanching the basil to help it keep its color. This would kill off the healthy bacteria in the basil that you are counting on for fermentation. But in theory, you should be able to blanch the basil and then adding a starter culture (page 24) to get fermentation going.

Something for Nothing

Here are some fun and tasty ways to use bits and scraps of fruits and vegetables that would otherwise end up in the compost or trash. There is no compromise in texture or flavor with these pickles, and you can give yourself a pat on the back for reducing your food waste while making good food. Plus, these something-for-nothing recipes are great party conversation starters.

Crunchy Kale Stem Relish

PREPARATION TIME: 35 minutes   OPTIONAL CANNING TIME: 10 minutes
WAIT TIME: 1 week, including 8- to 12-hour brining time   YIELD: Makes 4 half-pint jars

This is a delicious way to use those leaf midribs left over after you have stripped the "good" part away from kale leaves. The recipe can be multiplied, but the ingredient quantities here are good for the leafstalks left over from a typical store-bought bunch of kale. You can easily double or triple the pickling liquid quantities if you're bringing in a *lot* of kale from the garden.

Mix Crunchy Kale Stem Relish with quinoa or grains for a quick side dish. Or use it instead of Classic Hot Dog Relish (page 131) and enjoy the amazement when you tell people what they are actually eating.

INGREDIENTS

4 cups finely chopped kale leaf stalks (see Instructions)

2 large green bell peppers

2 medium large onions

2 tablespoons kosher or other non-iodized salt

1½ teaspoons cornstarch

½ cup cider vinegar

½ teaspoon whole celery seed

⅛ teaspoon freshly ground nutmeg

⅛ teaspoon freshly ground black pepper

¾ cup granulated sugar OR ½ cup light honey (orange blossom or clover honey works well)

INSTRUCTIONS

1. Wash the kale stalks. Hold each stalk at either end and bend until it snaps (just as you do when testing asparagus spears for their tender versus tough ends). Everything from the snap point to the skinnier tip is tender. Compost the rest.

2. Finely chop the tender kale leaf stalks, or pulse them a few times in a food processor. You want them to be minced, but not pureed.

3. Slice off the stem of the green bell peppers. Cut them in half and remove the seeds and any white pith. Peel the onions and slice off the ends. Finely chop the peppers and onions, or pulse them a few times in a food processor. As with the kale leaf stalks, you want them to be minced, but not pureed into mush.

4. Combine the kale stalks, green pepper, and onions in a large bowl. Add the salt and mix well. Don't worry if it seems like a lot of salt—you'll be rinsing most of it off in the next step. The salt will draw water out of the vegetables, which will result in better taste and texture in the finished relish.

5. Cover the bowl of salted vegetables and leave it in the refrigerator overnight or for 8 to 12 hours.

6. Put the vegetables into a finely meshed sieve and let them drain for a couple of minutes. Rinse them under cold water and then let them drain again for another minute or two. Press on the vegetables with the back of a wood spoon or your clean hands to remove as much liquid as possible.

7. In a large pot, whisk the cornstarch into the cider vinegar. Add the spices and sugar or honey. Bring the mixture to a boil over medium heat, stirring to dissolve the sugar or honey.

8. Once the spiced vinegar syrup is boiling, add the minced vegetables. Bring the mixture back to a boil, then reduce the heat and simmer, stirring occasionally, for 10 minutes.

9. Spoon the relish into clean hot canning jars. Press down on the relish with the back of a spoon or your clean fingers to release any air bubbles. Either screw on the lids and refrigerate immediately, or for long-term storage at room temperature, proceed to the next step.

10. Leave ½ inch of head space between the liquid and the top of the jar. Screw on the canning lids and process the relish in a boiling water bath (page 28) for 10 minutes. Adjust the canning time if you live at a high altitude. Once canned in a boiling water bath, the relish will keep inside the sealed jars at room temperature for at least a year. Once opened, the relish will keep in the refrigerator for up to 3 months.

11. Whether sealed by canning or simply refrigerated, wait at least a week for the flavors to mingle and develop before serving the relish.

Change It Up: Use broccoli stems or finely chopped cabbage cores instead of the kale. Use green tomatoes for a nice end-of-the-garden-season preserve.

Fruit Scrap Vinegar

PREPARATION TIME: 10 minutes, including daily stirring   WAIT TIME: 3 to 5 weeks   YIELD: Makes 1 pint

This is one of my favorite something-for-nothing recipes.

When you make applesauce, pie, or any apple recipe, save the cores (and the peels if the apples were organically grown). Or use the rind of a pineapple you just chopped up. Or banana peels. Or pretty much any fruit scrap you can think of that would otherwise be headed straight to the trash or (hopefully) compost.

Because this is a fermentation recipe, it is essential that the water you use be filtered (or non-chlorinated). Running the water through an ordinary pitcher filter such as Britta is sufficient.

It is also important that the fruit is organically grown. Since most of the scraps you use for this recipe will be the outer layer—peels, rinds, etc.—any pesticide or herbicide residue from conventionally (chemically) raised crops would end up in your homemade vinegar. Yuck. Start out with organically grown produce that was grown without toxic chemicals and this is not an issue.

Homemade vinegar is fantastic in salad dressings and marinades, but to use it to safely pickle food, see "How to Safely Use Homemade Vinegar in Pickling," page 26.

INGREDIENTS

3 tablespoons granulated sugar

3 cups filtered or unchlorinated water

1 pound fruit scraps (apple cores and peels, pineapple rinds, banana peels, pear cores, etc.)

INSTRUCTIONS

1. Dissolve the sugar in the water. Remember that it is important to use non-chlorinated or filtered water because chlorine could prevent the fermentation process that is essential to making vinegar.

2. Put the fruit scraps into a nonreactive bowl, pot, or crock (no aluminum, copper, or non-enameled cast iron) and pour the sugar water over them. Use enough of the liquid to cover the fruit scraps, but don't worry if they float a bit.

3. Cover with a clean dish towel and let sit at room temperature for 1 week. Every day, stir the ingredients vigorously at least once (more is better). Once fermentation begins, the liquid will froth up when you stir it.

4. The liquid should have started to turn a darker color after 1 week of steeping and stirring. Strain out the fruit scraps.

5. Keep the liquid at room temperature, stirring once or more each day, for 2 weeks to 1 month. Its smell will shift from lightly alcoholic to vinegar-y and sour. The bacteria that create vinegar from alcohol require oxygen to do their job. That's why it's important not to cover the liquid with anything airtight during the process. (FYI, *all* vinegar starts out as alcohol.)

6. Once the vinegar tastes as strong as you'd like it, transfer it to bottles and screw on covers or cork. The vinegar is fine to use for salad dressings, marinades, and sauces anytime it tastes good to you. But if you want to use your homemade vinegar for safe pickling and canning, it needs to have at least 4.5 percent acetic acid, just like commercial brands do (see "How to Safely Use Homemade Vinegar in Pickling," page 26).

Tip: You might think strawberry "hulls" (the green calyxes with a bit of fruit still attached) would be great candidates for fruit scrap vinegar. But for some reason, strawberries are more prone to mold than other fruits. You can still make a terrific strawberry scrap vinegar, but I recommend two things to fend off mold: 1) Stir the vinegar-in-progress at least four times a day, 2) Add a tablespoon of raw, unpasteurized vinegar once the fruit scraps are actively fermenting.

Fermented Beet (or Chard) Stems

PREPARATION TIME: 10 minutes   WAIT TIME: 3 days   YIELD: Makes 1 pint

You can't get any simpler than this two-ingredient, lacto-fermented pickle! The reason there is no salt added to prevent spoilage is that beet plants are naturally high in sodium, high enough to ensure a successful ferment even without added salt.

Although most people are more familiar with the beet root, beets also have a leafy green that you can, in turn, treat as two different vegetables. There is the green part, which is excellent raw or cooked. And then there are the thick, juicy, crisp leafstalks (sometimes called "ribs"). The latter is what we will use to make this ferment.

In this salt-free ferment, you can also use chard, sometimes called Swiss chard (except in Switzerland, where they find it amusing that we call it that). Any variety of chard will work. Rainbow chard, with its red, gold, and white leafstalks, makes a pretty and festive-looking ferment, but the plain white variety tastes just as good.

If you notice that the beet stems and the chard stems (of any color) taste identical, you are not hallucinating: Beets are the exact same species as chard (*Beta vulgaris*). In fact, beets are a variety of chard bred for its plump roots.

Lacto-fermented beet ribs are good on top of salads, but also when added at the last minute to soups. They are also excellent baked into casseroles with beans and feta cheese (if you don't mind losing some of the probiotic benefits to the oven heat).

INGREDIENTS

Leafstalks from one large bunch of beets (or chard)

Filtered or unchlorinated water

INSTRUCTIONS

1. Wash the beet leaves and slice off the green parts (save those for another use). Chop the beet leafstalks into ½- or 1-inch pieces.

2. Pack the beet stalks into a clean glass jar. Set the jar on a small plate. Pour the filtered or non-chlorinated water over the chard pieces. Fill the jar all the way to the rim, then place a lid on top. The lid will keep the beet stalk pieces submerged in the water, but you want it on loosely enough that gases can escape during fermentation.

3. Leave the jar of beet "ribs" at room temperature for 24 hours. After that, take off the lid and check for signs of fermentation. Within 24 to 72 hours, you should see some bubbles or foam on the surface of the liquid, and the beets will start to have the characteristic light sour smell of a fresh fermentation. Leave the beets at room temperature until they are clearly fermenting. During the 1 to 3 days that will take, keep the jar topped up with filtered or non-chlorinated water at all times.

4. Once fermentation has been underway for a couple days, seal the lid tightly. Put the lacto-fermented beet stalks into the refrigerator or a cold cellar.

They will keep, chilled, for at least 6 months but the texture is best if it is eaten within 3 months. Note that white chard leafstalks sometimes darken when they are fermented, especially the pieces in the top half of the jar. This is harmless, and they will still taste good.

Change It Up: Like beets and chard, celery is naturally high in salt and can be safely fermented with the addition of nothing but water. Substitute celery for beets or chard in this recipe; just remember that the water must be filtered or non-chlorinated for a successful fermentation.

Tip: If the ambient temperature where you are leaving the beet or chard stalks to ferment is above 75°F, add a pinch of kosher or other non-iodized salt. This will prevent the spoilage that is more likely to occur in hot weather.

Pickled Asparagus Ends (Not Tips)

PREPARATION TIME: 15 minutes   WAIT TIME: 3 days   YIELD: Makes 3 (approximately) half-pint jars

The usual instruction for fresh asparagus is to hold either end of one spear and bend until it snaps: everything from the snapping point to the tip is tender, and what is left of the other end is usually discarded.

Not so fast! The tough part of the base ends of asparagus spears mainly lies in the skin and in the fibrous area just below the skin. Peel that off, and what you've got is good, tender asparagus that can be beautifully preserved as a refrigerator pickle.

Note that this pickle does not contain enough vinegar for boiling water bath canning and must be treated as a refrigerator pickle.

INGREDIENTS

3½ pounds asparagus spears

1 pint filtered or unchlorinated water

½ cup white wine vinegar

1 tablespoon kosher or other non-iodized salt

1 tablespoon granulated sugar OR agave nectar

1 teaspoon whole black peppercorns

½ teaspoon whole dill seeds

3 garlic cloves, lightly smashed

6 whole allspice

½ teaspoon red pepper flakes OR 1 small hot chile pepper (optional)

INSTRUCTIONS

1. Bend each asparagus spear until it snaps. Set aside the tender tip ends for another recipe. Cut any dry bases off the other ends of the asparagus. Peel the trimmed base ends with a vegetable peeler. Chop the pieces into approximately uniform lengths.

2. Bring the water, vinegar, salt, and sugar or honey to a boil, stirring occasionally to dissolve the salt and sugar. While you are waiting for the pickling liquid to come to a boil, put the peppercorns, dill seeds, garlic, allspice, and optional red pepper flakes into a clean heatproof jar. If using the whole chile pepper instead of the pepper flakes, pierce it with the tip of a knife before adding it to the jar.

3. Load the jar with the peeled asparagus pieces. It will be easier to keep the pieces all lined up the same way if you initially load the jar while it is on its side. Keep packing the asparagus into the jar until you can't squeeze in even one more piece.

4. Pour the hot brine over the asparagus and spices. The liquid should completely cover the asparagus pieces. If any are floating to the surface, tuck a grape vine leaf or piece of a cabbage leaf over the asparagus like a blanket. The leaf will keep the asparagus submerged in the pickling liquid.

5. Lightly tap the bottom of the jar on a dish towel-lined countertop to release any air bubbles. Affix the lid. Let the pickles cool to room temperature before transferring them to the refrigerator or another cold but not freezing place.

6. Wait at least 3 days for the flavors to develop before sampling.

Change It Up: Cut kohlrabi into French fry-shaped sticks and use these instead of the asparagus. Add fresh dill or fennel leaves to the jar.

Tip: Serve these pickled asparagus ends as part of a chopped salad. Or try them chopped and added to potato or egg salads.

Pickled Watermelon Rind

PREPARATION TIME: 45 minutes   OPTIONAL CANNING TIME: 10 minutes
WAIT TIME: 2 weeks, plus 8 to 12 hours initial brining time   YIELD: Makes 3 pints

This something-for-nothing recipe takes a part of the watermelon that we usually toss away—the whitish layer between the green rind and the sweet red flesh—and turns it into wonderful food.

For the best results with watermelon rind pickles, choose an old-fashioned variety that still has seeds and a white rind layer at least ½ inch thick. Seedless varieties tend to have rinds too thin to bother with.

I like to leave just a sliver of the pink-red part on for its color. The white rind has a better texture for pickling, but it never hurts to include a little eye candy.

INGREDIENTS

4 pounds watermelon rinds, weighed after removing the green rinds (leave no more than ⅛ inch of the pink part attached)

¼ cup kosher or other non-iodized salt

1 quart plus 1½ cups filtered or unchlorinated water

1½ cups cider vinegar OR unseasoned rice vinegar

1 cup granulated sugar

3 cinnamon sticks

3 whole cloves

3 whole allspice

1 lemon, cut into thin slices, peel still attached (be sure to use an organic lemon—you don't want pesticides along with that peel, do you?)

INSTRUCTIONS

1. Cut the watermelon rind into pieces 1 to 2 inches long and between ½ and ¾ inch thick.

2. Dissolve the salt in 1 quart of the water and pour over the watermelon rind pieces in a large bowl. Refrigerate for 8 hours or as long as 12 hours.

3. Drain the watermelon rind pieces in a colander, rinse under cool water, and drain again.

4. Put the watermelon into a nonreactive pot (no aluminum, copper, or non-enameled cast iron), along with the remaining water and rest of the ingredients, and bring to a boil over medium-high heat, stirring to dissolve the sugar.

5. Reduce the heat and simmer until the watermelon rind pieces are translucent, 20 to 30 minutes.

6. With a slotted spoon, transfer the watermelon rind into clean canning jars, leaving at least 1 inch of head space. As you load in the watermelon, tuck one of the cinnamon sticks and a few of the lemon slices into each jar.

7. Pour the pickling liquid over the watermelon. The watermelon rinds should be completely covered by the pickling liquid with at least ½ inch of head space remaining.

8. Secure the lids and either refrigerate immediately or process in a boiling water bath (page 28) for 10 minutes. Adjust the canning time if you live at a high altitude.

9. Wait at least 2 weeks before serving.

Tip: You can stockpile watermelon rinds in the refrigerator for up to 3 days before making this recipe. Don't freeze them though, or their texture when thawed will be too squishy for pickling.

Pickled Radish Leaf Pesto

PREPARATION TIME: 5 to 10 minutes   WAIT TIME: Ready to eat immediately; will keep, refrigerated, for at least 1 month   YIELD: Makes approximately 1 cup

Most people don't realize that radish leaves are just as edible as their roots. This spicy, tangy paste can replace prepared mustard in sandwiches and pretty much any other dish.

INGREDIENTS

2 tablespoons extra virgin olive oil

½ pound radish leaves

⅓ cup vinegar

3 garlic cloves

½ teaspoon kosher or other non-iodized salt

INSTRUCTIONS

1. Heat the olive oil in a skillet over medium heat. Add the radish leaves and cook, stirring, until the leaves are completely wilted.

2. Put the cooked radish leaves together with the vinegar, garlic, and salt in a blender or food processor. Puree the ingredients to a smooth paste.

3. Put the radish leaf pesto into a clean glass jar. Pour additional olive oil in, enough to completely cover the surface of the radish leaf paste with oil. The vinegar has already killed off any harmful bacteria; now the oil layer keeps out mold spores from the air. Store in the refrigerator or another cold but not freezing place.

*Change It Up: Add grated cheese and crushed walnuts before serving. Use mustard, or garlic mustard (*Alliaria petiolata*) greens instead of the radish leaves. Try chives or wild garlic instead of the garlic.*

Tip: Add more olive oil as needed each time you scoop out some of the radish leaf pesto. The pesto should always be completely covered by the oil.

No matter how well you understand the food safety principles, how carefully you follow the recipe, and how meticulously you choose your ingredients, sometimes things go wrong. The good news is that most pickling predicaments are either harmless or preventable. Read on and don't panic: you got this.

Help! My Garlic Turned Blue

Pickled garlic will sometimes turn blue. This is the result of an enzymatic reaction that occurs occasionally when the sulfur compounds in garlic are exposed to oxygen and then to an acidic environment, such as a vinegar-based pickle brine. The

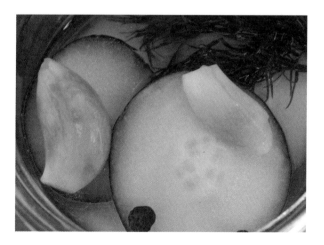

bright blue color may seem alarming, but actually, it is harmless, and the pickles—including the blue garlic—are still perfectly safe to eat.

Mushy Pickles

Crunch defines many pickles just as much as the tangy taste, so it's no fun when your pickles turn out to be mushy. There's no way to restore a firm texture to a pickle that has already gone soft, but there are ways to slant the odds in your favor for the crisp consistency you're after.

The single most important thing is the quality of the ingredients you start out with. An overgrown, seedy, limp cucumber cannot ever turn into a crunchy pickle. Always start out with firm, unblemished vegetables or fruit for the best pickles. This usually means younger and smaller vegetables (the less-than-an-inch-thick zucchini, not the giant supermarket type). Got less than perfect produce to work with? Opt for a finely chopped or pureed recipe such as a chutney, relish, or ketchup rather than pickling large pieces that will disappoint.

The next mush-preventing thing to do is to slice off a sliver of the flower end of vegetables, especially cucumbers. This end can contain enzymes whose job it is in nature to speed the decay of the fruit and the release of its seeds. (Scientifically, a "fruit" is simply the seed-bearing part of a plant. Since cucumbers have seeds, they are technically fruits. So are zucchini, green beans, etc.). Leaving the flower end of a cucumber or other vegetable intact with those enzymes can result in mushy pickles. Not sure which end was the flower end? Hedge your bet by slicing a sliver off both ends.

With fermented pickles, transferring them from room temperature to the refrigerator, or from a loosely covered jar to a tightly closed one, before active fermentation is complete, can result in mushy pickles. You have to choose your battles. On the one hand, a ferment that moves to the refrigerator early on is going to have a lighter, less sour taste than one that spent a few more weeks on your counter. And that can be a good thing. On the other hand, you could end up with a softer pickle. That is especially true with cucumber pickles such as the Half Sours on page 65. And remember that all fermented pickles will soften somewhat the longer you store them.

Last but not least, you can add ingredients that preserve crunchiness. (It is worth repeating that you cannot *add* crunchiness. You can only preserve it in ingredients that are already crisp.) Calcium chloride and alum are frequently sold for this purpose in pickling, but I am not a fan of these (see "Ingredients," page 35). The better idea is to tuck a high-tannin leaf such as a grape vine, oak, or cherry tree leaf into each jar of pickles.

Lacto-Fermentation Foes

FERMENTATION NEVER BEGINS, OR THE FOOD SPOILS EVEN AFTER FERMENTATION SEEMED TO START

If, after 1 to 3 days at a room temperature somewhere between 60°F to 85°F, your ferment still hasn't started fermenting, you may have to compost it and start over. Definitely, if the food smells bad (it should have a lightly sour smell when fermenting, not a rotten one), or if there are strings of cloudy muck in the liquid, the batch has spoiled and should be discarded. Note that mold is *not* necessarily a reason to abandon your ferment (see below).

Two things that can help prevent a non-starting ferment or a spoiled one are adjusting the amount of salt according to the ambient temperature and/or including a live culture starter from whey (such as that from strained yogurt, page 24).

MOLD ON TOP OF FERMENTS

It is not uncommon for mold to form on top of ferments. The two most common steps for preventing it are as follows: You can hold the solid ingredients down under the liquid with a weight (or a leaf blanket). Or, you can stir the ferment vigorously at least once a day.

But it is important to know that not all molds are dangerous. In fact, you've probably eaten them on purpose (blue cheese, anyone?). If I find a white mold on the surface of my fermenting chile peppers, for example, I usually just scrape it off with a spoon and eat the peppers without fear. But if I were to find black mold (the dangerous kind) on top of my pepper ferment (this has never happened to me, but if it did . . .), I would toss that entire batch and sterilize the container. Black mold is the dangerous kind: don't mess with it.

Canning Woes

JARS THAT DON'T SEAL

There are four main reasons why a canning jar may fail to seal after boiling water bath or pressure canning.

Over-filling the jars: if you left less than the amount of head space specified by the recipe, a good vacuum seal won't form. If the recipe instructions don't specify an amount of head space (the space between the surface of the food and the rim of the jar), then between ½ and ¾ inch is a good all-purpose distance to aim for. This also happens to be approximately the distance between the rim of the jar and the ridges just below its screw band area, which makes it easy to measure.

The next reason why a jar may not seal is that there was some food or liquid on the rim of the jar. This can prevent the adhesive ring on the underside of the lid from fastening onto the jar. To prevent this from happening, always wipe the rims of the jars clean after you have filled them with the food you are canning. Use a moist, clean cloth or paper towel.

The third reason a jar may fail to seal is that the canning lid is defective. This can happen with new lids—it is rare, but it does happen. More likely is that someone tried to reuse a canning lid. With two-piece lids, you can reuse the screw-on ring, but you are not supposed to reuse the central disk. Single-piece lids are not supposed to be reused at all. The reason is that previous use may have worn out the adhesive ring, or there may be some barely noticeable dent or bend that could prevent a seal. It is not dangerous to reuse a canning lid, so long as you pay attention to whether or not it has sealed. But you could waste time preparing a recipe that then has to be re-canned or refrigerated. Never store an unsealed canning jar with moist food inside at room temperature. That is only for sealed jars.

The last reason why a jar may not seal is that there is a tiny chip or crack in the rim of the jar. Always carefully examine each jar before using it, and recycle any jars that have chips or cracks. This is especially true of jars you have reused many times, or that you purchased secondhand from a garage sale or thrift shop.

A JAR BREAKS IN PROCESSING

You open the canner to find broken glass and food floating in the hot water. Or everything looks fine until you reach in with your jar lifter to lift one out, and the entire bottom drops off of the jar. Not fun. Here are the three possible explanations of what went wrong, and how to prevent a repeat experience.

The most likely culprit is a hairline crack in the jar that you didn't notice when you got it out for your

WHAT TO DO WITH A JAR THAT DIDN'T SEAL:

You took the jars out of the canner, and as they cooled, all but one of them sealed. What do you do with that unsealed jar? You have two options. The first is to simply store it in the refrigerator immediately and eat the contents within a week. The second is to reprocess the jar with a new lid. To do this, you'll need to first empty the jar, reheat the contents to a boil, clean the jar, and refill it with the food. Be sure to leave enough head space, wipe the rim of the jar clean, and use a fresh lid before reprocessing in a boiling water bath or pressure canner according to the recipe instructions. Keep in mind that when food is heat-processed more than once, both its nutritional content and quality of texture and taste decline.

These two ways of handling an unsealed jar only apply to jars that were freshly canned. It's a different story if a jar was originally sealed, but isn't sealed any more when you take it off the shelf weeks or months later. The best response in this case is to throw the food out.

canning project. As I mentioned in the unsealed jars notes above, always inspect jars to make sure they are free from cracks or chips before using them.

Another possibility is too sudden a temperature shift. Although canning jars are designed to withstand high heat, if they are cold when you pour in boiling hot food, or the jar and the food in it are hot but the water in the canner is cold, or there is any other sudden jolt from hot to cold or vice versa, the jar may crack. Often this will be a hard-to-spot hairline crack that you won't notice until the jar breaks during processing. Always fill empty jars with hot water to heat them, then pour the water out before adding hot food. Make sure the water in the canner is equally hot before adding the jars of hot food.

One last reason why jars could break during boiling water bath or pressure canning is that you didn't put a rack or towel in the bottom of the canner before adding the jars. The jars bounce around a bit during processing and need a buffer between the glass jar bottoms and both the metal bottom of the canner and the heat source directly under it. If you follow the boiling water bath canning instructions on page 28, this won't be an issue.

THE FOOD FLOATED OUT OF THE PICKLING LIQUID

The green beans floated up out of their preserving liquid during boiling water bath canning, or the chile peppers are floating on top of their brine. Even if the jar is sealed, the pickles are now partially out of the liquid. None of these scenarios are attractive in the jars. Worse yet, the vegetables or fruit pieces that rose above their pickling liquid into the head space between that and the lid may turn brown. Yuck.

With all types of pickles, it is essential that the food is completely immersed in the brine or vinegar-based pickling liquid. So how do you accomplish that?

The first solution, if you are dealing with relatively long pieces of food you are going to stack vertically in the jars, such as green beans, carrots, whole cucumbers, or zucchini spears, is to be sure to pack the food in tightly. Really tightly. Keep shoving the pieces in until you can't find room for even one more. This is especially important for recipes that start out with raw vegetables in the jars, because the vegetables will shrink quite a bit during fermentation or canning.

The next solution is to put something on top of the pickles to keep the food submerged in the liquid. In the case of fermented pickles, you can use a weight such as the fitted ones that fermentation crocks come supplied with. Or improvise one with a plate on top of the fermenting food with something heavy on it, such as a clean stone.

Yet another method is to use a piece of a large, edible leaf such as cabbage, kale, grape vine, or horseradish. Put the leaf on top of the pickles in the jar like a little blanket. Use a chopstick to tuck the edges of the leaf down between the pickles and the inside of the jar.

ACKNOWLEDGMENTS

During the first months of working on this book, I was in the middle of yoga teacher training. Once a week we trainees were supposed to contribute something to a potluck lunch. Because I was testing recipes for this book, my contribution was almost always pickles. Many thanks to Roxi, Boaz, Asaf, and all my fellow yogis at Yoga Mala for enthusiastically gobbling up my pickled offerings.

Thanks to Hank Shaw for his Tabasco sauce research, and to Pascal Baudar for the reminder about pickled seeds.

During the last months of working on this book, I was living in a campervan with my husband, Ricky Orbach, traveling through Mexico and Central America. You may notice inspiration from those travels in some of the recipes in this book. But the most constant motivator was my vanmate. Thank you, my love, for your deep enjoyment of my food when I get it right, and your honesty when I don't.

Thanks to Roey Orbach for the photographic assistance, and Raz Orbach for letting me steal one of his beers to use in the pickled carambola recipe. Thanks also to Ruchi Orbach and Maya Orbach for much kitchen assistance, and to Sharon Quarters for the photo setup.

Kendall Cornell and Francis Patrelle will recognize some of their kitchen gear in a few of the photos: thank you for once again being such gracious hosts.

Thanks to Avishai Goldberg and Efrat Mazor for the Persian wedding pickle (both making it and photographing it). I promise it has nothing to do with the sourness or sweetness of marriage, but everything to do with celebrating with friends and family (consider that an open invite, but you already knew that).

Many thanks to Ellen Zachos for the pickled pine nuts photo. What would a Leda Meredith book be without an Ellen Zachos photo?

And thanks to Michael O'Connor for the fermented green cherry tomatoes photo. How fun that you found my recipe and made the tomatoes before you realized you knew the author!

The writing of this book ended as it began, with a yoga intensive. This time, during the final days before submitting the manuscript, I was studying with Julie Dohrman in Costa Rica. And once again, thanks to my fellow yogis for their enthusiastic feedback on my pickles.

BOOKS AND WEBSITES

The Art of Fermentation: An In-depth Exploration of Essential Concepts and Processes from Around the World, by Sandor Ellix Katz

> Sandor's follow up to *Wild Fermentation*. If you want to voyage down the rabbit hole of the science and how-to's of different forms of fermentation, this is your new bestie.

Hot Chile Peppers on the Scoville Scale

> Want to know if the chile peppers you're about to add to your kimchi are going to contribute a slight tingle or a blow-your-socks-off-burn? This list will make it clear. https://www.thespruce.com/hot-chile-peppers-scoville-scale-1807552

Food in Jars and *Preserving by the Pint: Quick Seasonal Canning for Small Spaces*, by Marisa McClellan

> Excellent recipes and advice for those (like me) who live in tiny homes or apartments. Not exclusively about pickling, but many excellent pickle recipes are included.

National Center for Home Food Preservation

> This site provides clear, frequently updated information on safe food preservation procedures, including canning times, adjustments for altitude, etc. I'm not a big fan of their recipes, but if you need to look up how much longer you need to can that quart of pickles as compared to a pint, etc., this is a great resource. http://nchfp.uga.edu/

The New Wildcrafted Cuisine: Exploring the Exotic Gastronomy of Local Terroir, by Pascal Baudar

> Although not exclusively about pickling or food preservation, this beautiful wild foods book explores both. It includes excellent instructions for making your own fermented sodas and vinegars.

Nourishing Traditions: The Cookbook That Challenges Politically Correct Nutrition and the Diet Dictocrats, by Sally Fallon

> The inspiration for some of my favorite lacto-fermentation recipes originally came from this book. But be prepared to have some of your nutritional beliefs challenged!

Preserving Everything

> By the author of this book, *Preserving Everything* includes information and recipes on food preservation methods, including dehydrating, pressure canning, dry salting, and preserv-

ing in alcohol, as well as both fermented and vinegar-based pickles.

Wild Fermentation

Both the website and Sandor Ellix Katz's book of the same name are fantastic sources of information on all things fermented. https://www.wildfermentation.com/

GEAR AND INGREDIENTS

Acid Titration Kit

Although the instructions that come with this easy-to-use kit are for home winemakers, you can use it along with the instructions on page 26 to test the acidity of your homemade vinegar. Most online winemaking sites offer these kits.

Black Walnuts

The flavor of black walnuts is entirely different from those of the English walnuts commonly sold in the United States. If you can't forage any near you, here's a source. https://nuts.com/nuts/walnuts/black.html

Canning Jars, Jar Lifters, Canning Funnels, etc.

You can usually find these at your local hardware or housewares store, but if you need to order by mail, this is a good source: https://www.freshpreserving.com/

Fermentation Crocks

Stone Creek Trading has a variety of sizes of ceramic fermentation crocks with fitted weights. https://www.stonecreektrading.com/collections/fermenting

pH Meter

Use this when you've invented a new pickle recipe and want to confirm whether it is acidic enough for boiling water bath canning, or if it needs to be treated as a refrigerator pickle. pH meters are available from numerous online sources.

Spicebush

I mention this as an alternative to allspice and black pepper in several recipes. I am completely enamored with this native spice (*Lindera benzoin*). If it doesn't grow where you live, or you are not planning to forage for it yourself, you can order it from Integration Acres. Just be aware that they label it as "Appalachian Allspice." https://integrationacres.com/

Xanthum Gum

This keeps your homemade hot sauce from separating. You only need a tiny amount per bottle of sauce, so one order of this lasts a long time. You can get xanthum gum from big online sellers such as Amazon, but I prefer to order directly from Bob's Red Mill. https://www.bobsredmill.com/

INDEX

Leda Meredith is the author of several books, including *Preserving Everything: Can, Culture, Pickle, Freeze, Ferment, Dehydrate, Salt, Smoke, and Store Fruits, Vegetables, Milk, Meat, and More*; *The Forager's Feast: How to Identify, Harvest, and Prepare Wild Edibles*; and *Northeast Foraging: 120 Wild and Flavorful Edibles from Beach Plums to Wineberries*. She holds a certification in Ethnobotany from the New York Botanical Garden where she has been an instructor since 2002. She also teaches at the Brooklyn Botanical Garden and for numerous organizations internationally. You can find out more about Leda's edible and botanical adventures and sign up for her classes at www.ledameredith.com and watch her food instruction videos at www.youtube.com/ledameredith. You can also follow her on Facebook, Twitter, Instagram, and Pinterest (she's ledameredith on all of them).